D1458207

C153787451

Twenty Days
in the
Reich

Twenty Days
in the
Reich

Three Downed RAF Aircrew in Germany during 1945

Flying Officer Squire 'Tim' Scott

Pen & Sword
AVIATION

This edition first published in Great Britain in 2006
By Pen & Sword Aviation
An imprint of Pen and Sword Books Ltd
47 Church Street
Barnsley
South Yorkshire
S70 2AS

ISBN 1 84415 390 8
     1 84415 333 6

A CIP record for this book is available from the British
Library.

Typeset in the UK by Mac Style, Nafferton, E. Yorkshire
Printed and bound in the UK by CPI UK.

Pen & Sword Books Ltd incorporates the imprints of Pen &
Sword Aviation, Pen & Sword Maritime, Pen & Sword
Military, Wharncliffe Local History, Pen & Sword Select,
Pen & Sword Military Classics and Leo Cooper.

For a complete list of Pen & Sword titles please contact
Pen & Sword Books Limited
47 Church Street, Barnsley, South Yorkshire, S70 2AS,
England
E-mail: enquiries@pen-and-sword.co.uk
Website: www.pen-and-sword.co.uk

Dedication

To the American Third Army

Contents

Foreword

This is not an escape story. It is therefore just a little bit different from the many excellent narrative accounts of the breath-taking adventures of those who eluded their Nazi guards and made their way back, unaided or otherwise, to their own lines.

This tale then, is one, simply told, of the experiences of three members of the crew of a Bomber Command Lancaster who baled out of their crippled aircraft on Thursday 15 March 1945. They were actually prisoners-of-war for fifteen days out of twenty-two spent on the continent of Europe, although their time behind the barbed wire was limited to a bare thirty-six hours.

If any of their several attempts to escape had been successful, this would just be another escape story and, in any case, would probably never have been written. Some part of the author's purpose will have been achieved, if the reader gains just a tiny insight into what went on 'over the other side' during those history-making days of March and April 1945.

CHAPTER ONE

Captured

Oil had been leaking from the Lancaster port inboard engine practically from the moment that we had crossed the French coast on that memorable March afternoon.

A huge anticyclone had covered the whole of the British Isles and most of Europe and for several days the weather had been gloriously fine. The weather not only gave us our third 'op' in successive days, but also played an important part in the miracle of our liberation that was to follow.

It was our thirty-first sortie and that morning, as we had strolled around the dispersal, chatting to the ground crew in those tense few minutes before it was time to taxi out to the end of the runway, we had groused mildly at the working of the minds of those 'high ups'. Only a few days before, they had thought fit to increase the number of trips in a tour from thirty to thirty-six.

We reflected that, but for this display of inconsideration, we should have finished our tour yesterday. However, we were not unduly dismayed, because with the weather as it was, we did not think that it would be long before we were enjoying our well-earned fortnight's 'end of tour' leave. I remember my leg being pulled, because although I had always declined to join the rest of the crew in their occasional drinking orgies, I promised them faithfully that on this auspicious event I would get as drunk as any of them!

Both Jack, our rear-gunner, and Roy, the mid-upper gunner, noticed the oil at a very early stage of the trip and the Skipper had accepted the information with his usual polite calm. We knew our Skipper well and whilst later on we had plenty of time to reflect that some captains on the squadron might, quite legitimately have put the port inboard engine out of use (an operation known as feathering, which if implemented soon enough can render an engine ineffective and yet perfectly harmless), dropped the bomb in the Channel and returned to base on three engines, I doubt if any of us expected or wanted such a decision from him.

I recalled the occasion when all my secret equipment had packed up on a long night-stooge operation to Munich. I can still hear the Skipper's almost ghoulish chuckle when he told me that I now had a golden opportunity to display my skill at ordinary dead reckoning navigation. As the latter consists mainly of paper and pencil theory, I knew that the Skipper was as well aware as I was, that our chances of even being able to locate the distant target were not promising.

No, as long as there was any chance of reaching the target, we knew that we should press on. Although reports were coming through from the rear that the whole of the back portion of the aircraft was covered in oil from the faulty engine, we suffered no loss of speed. We duly reached our objective, which was near the town of Arnsberg, in the eastern Ruhr area, on time and in our correct place in the formation.

We unloaded our single $5\frac{1}{2}$-ton bomb, with our blessing for any unfortunate Germans who might happen to be directly underneath. We had flown about ten minutes on the homeward journey when the fun commenced. Arthur, the engineer, announced that the port inner engine would have to be feathered, as the gauges were showing hardly any oil content. The revolutions were already building up far beyond their maximum.

'Go on then, have a go and see if she'll feather', came the Skipper's matter-of-fact voice over the intercom. Now that we were rid of our great bomb load, the loss of one engine would not be serious. Even at that stage I had no suspicion of any immediate danger, even if the faulty engine should fail to feather. The last entry in my log read '1650 – port inner unserviceable …'. I had then left a short space in which, as I thought, to insert 'feathered' or otherwise as the case might be.

Arthur's voice came up as placid as his captain's, 'It's no use Skip, she won't feather –

she's batting round like the devil and will be on fire in two ticks if we don't look out.'

The Skipper's voice came over the intercom, still completely unperturbed. He was calling up the formation leader and informing him of the emergency in our aircraft. The next words I heard were 'Fix parachutes'.

Mechanically, I obeyed and acknowledged the order. It seemed almost like a training exercise. The only coherent thought that I can recollect was that it was going to be exceedingly awkward grappling with my navigation instruments with a parachute fixed to my chest.

'OK. Jump!' This order seemed to come in less than a minute. I heard a startled 'Jump?' from some unknown member of the crew, but did not stop for any more.

I was delayed a few seconds as my telephone lines and oxygen tube became entangled. I can still see the terribly anxious look on the Skipper's face as eventually I slipped past him on my way to the front hatch.

Never in the whole of my time in the RAF had the value of training and discipline been more forcibly presented to me. I didn't think about it then of course – all I did was sit with my ripcord handle well clutched, over the absurdly small hole in the floor, duck my head and in no time at all I was in the nice, clear, blue air!

But a lot of things came to me later on. Aircrew of course, contrary to popular belief, do not practise parachute jumping. Unlike an airborne trooper, whose job depends on his skill at 'baling out', we were trained to regard a jump as a purely last line of defence – to be used in an absolute emergency. One's first effort, would, one hoped, be the only one that would ever be necessary during a whole flying career.

What we had done, though, was to practise the whole thing into a sheet from a height of about 8 feet. I can honestly say that I never came across a man who would believe, without it being proved to him, that it was possible to get through that hole *in the manner laid down*, without cracking his skull on the far side of it.

The hatch is roughly 2 feet square and the prescribed manner is to sit on the backward edge, legs dangling, fold the hands across the chest, drop the head forward and perform a neat somersault, head first into space.

Everyone, little fellows as well as big, was convinced that he was sure to bang his head on the forward edge of the hole. Demonstrations soon proved otherwise, and in a little while each trainee was mustering sufficient courage to satisfy himself that not only could it be done, but that this was the only way to do it. Merely to drop out feet first would be to run the almost certain risk of hitting some part of the upper body on the edge of the hatch, as the force of the slipstream would drag the legs backwards far more quickly than the trunk would leave the aircraft.

I still chuckle to myself when I think of one poor chap who was particularly apprehensive of this practice leap into the sheet. Two crews used to go on at a time, taking it in turns to hold the sheet for each other. That morning, thirteen of us had made two or three practice leaps each, satisfying ourselves beyond all doubt that it could be done, and we could do it.

This young Scottish engineer, however, could not be persuaded to make the attempt. It was nearing lunch time, he was up in the aircraft looking as forlorn as could be, and we were all standing below, egging him on to have a go. Finally, our Skipper went back and up through the aircraft. He approached the hole, and without even pausing on the edge, he made the leap to illustrate how simple it really was.

We thought that this had done the trick. The engineer seated himself on the vacant position on the hatch – he took off his collar and tie and pitched them into the sheet. His cigarette lighter, watch, fountain pen and spare change followed at short intervals. The half a dozen men holding the sheet made all ready – surely something was going to happen now! At last, when the tension was becoming unbearable, the hapless victim extracted his false teeth from his mouth and with a final gesture of despair tossed them amid his other possessions.

It may not sound as funny as it looked, but the entire team of sheet bearers collapsed in helpless laughter on the ground. When they had recovered, a further attempt was made, but it was of no avail. The best that the chap could be persuaded to do was to lower himself gingerly into the sheet in the manner of a novice swimmer getting into a pool.

It was a good laugh at the time, but I'll wager it would not have seemed so funny at 12,000 feet over enemy territory, with perhaps three or four of one's comrades waiting to get out of a doomed aircraft. That is why I was so thankful for my training, because I am certain that if I had had to sit on the edge of that hole and weigh up whether or not I could get through in the correct way, then I should have been seated there for a jolly sight longer than would have been comfortable for myself or for anybody else.

I am still quite amazed when I recollect how short seemed to be the interval that elapsed between sitting on the edge of the hatch, and drifting in the fresh blue air. I think I must have pulled my ripcord straight away, in which case, according to the rules and regulations, I ought not to have survived, as the parachute should have become caught up with some part of the aircraft. I suppose, though, counting to three or five or whatever it is (I was never quite sure) must ensure a margin of safety far in excess of what is necessary. I do know that quite a few men have told me that they allowed themselves quite a long period of dropping like a stone, just to see what it felt like! They are far braver men than I, I am afraid.

My first coherent thought as I floated down was of the utter parlousness of my plight, but this was followed immediately afterwards by the realisation that I was immensely lucky to be still alive and in one piece. I offered a silent prayer to my Maker for my safety in the unknown future that was before me.

The apparent blueness of the air on this brilliant spring day, and the complete peace and quiet that reigned after the noise of the aircraft, are phenomena that have been reported many times before. I was struck, too, by the colossal distance that the ground seemed below me (I jumped from about 12,000 feet so would probably have been about 10,000 feet, or just under 2 miles high, at the time of this observation), but at no time afterwards was I able to give anyone any idea of how long it took me to complete the descent. I have learnt since that it must have been about five minutes.

After trying to look upwards to see if anyone was above me, and finding that I could see little but the immense expanse of my canopy, I began to study the layout below. I at once saw a parachute flattening out in what looked like open country far below. I decided that this must belong to Ron, the bomb-aimer, who would have been sitting practically on the escape hatch. He was also one of the slickest men I ever knew at moving in an emergency. Poor Ron was my best friend and, as I write, he is the only one of the crew of seven about whom we still have no news.

Soon afterwards, I spotted two more 'chutes drifting earthwards. I made a careful survey of the land below so that I could, if I were lucky enough to get away, make towards some part of the countryside where I might pick up a companion. At what would be about 1000 feet above the 'deck', I discovered that this was a wasted effort because the landscape devolved itself into a series of valleys surrounded by fairly high hills and all three of the other parachutes disappeared into folds in the ground. 'So that's that', I reflected rather dismally.

A quick glance below told me that it was getting very near my time. I seemed to be almost immediately over a very small village and I could already discern bodies appearing from around corners and making for a common meeting point. Somewhat belatedly, I began to check up on my landing 'gen'. The knees should be kept well together and allowed to collapse sideways just as the feet touched the ground. The automatic locking device on the parachute should be in the 'danger' position just before making contact, so as to ensure a speedy release from the harness if the parachute should start to blow away. We had practised all this on a dummy set-up in a hangar, but I had a feeling of rustiness that I had not experienced with the jump itself.

The feeling was intensified a few seconds later when I looked down again and saw, that with probably only 100 feet to fall, I was right over the roof tops. Simultaneously, I perceived that the strength of the advancing villagers was such that my hope of escape was nil. I'm afraid my drill went a bit haywire; desperately, I clutched at all the ropes I could get my hands on and pulled them in all directions in an effort to make myself go anywhere but on those menacing-looking houses. It was just a matter of seconds, and then – with a huge thrill of relief – I realised I was just clearing the last house, then over the hedge lining a lane. The next moment I had settled comfortably, and with no undue concussion, into the comparative softness of a newly ploughed field.

All the rest of the drill had come out automatically and I soon discovered that I was quite unhurt, except for a slight scratch on the chin, which had probably caught a stone. The first batch of the population arrived as I sorted myself out and looked around. My only concern at that moment was to make sure that nobody thought that I was going to be awkward. At that stage in the proceedings there was obviously little future in such a policy. Accordingly, as I scrambled to my feet, I pulled my handkerchief out of my pocket and waved it on the air, my other hand being aloft also.

This seemed to be understood; a man with a pitchfork parked it peaceably under his arm. A quick search was made to see if I carried arms, which I did not. The next minute, the centre of an awe-stricken mob, I was led away through a gap in the hedge and down the lane to a building that seemed already allocated for my reception.

CHAPTER TWO

To Gaol

As I strolled slowly along the lane with my captors, I could not help being struck by the extreme beauty of this tiny German hamlet. I was also impressed with the friendly attitude of the inhabitants. I was to learn, but not until several days later, how fortunate I was not to have alighted somewhere that had recently suffered the effects of Allied bombing. In such towns, the reception was liable to be very different.

A priest came up to me, smiling amicably, and explained in quite good English that he was a Roman Catholic; he was not in the least disappointed when I told him that I was not. Little boys and girls grinned at me with obvious sympathy for my situation. Altogether, I got the impression that I could not have been more welcome had I come down in France, Belgium or some other friendly land!

We soon reached the building, which might have been a farm or a public house. I could not be sure which, as at that stage of my acquaintance with the Fatherland, I had developed no sense of distinction between their various odd-looking structures. I sank thankfully into a chair that was offered to me. I suppose I must have looked a trifle pale and careworn, for I could feel that a reaction had begun to set in. At any rate, a woman brought me a glass of pale pink liquid that might have been anything from disinfectant to methylated spirits, but which I charitably assumed was meant to be wine. When she followed this with a glass of fresh milk (the first and last I ever saw in Germany) my wilted body began rapidly to revive.

I suppose half an hour passed whilst I sat there, listening to the unintelligible jabber. The only interlude that affected me was when a particularly uncouth-looking rustic appeared, brandishing a revolver. His manner and excited speech indicated that something had happened that had somewhat soured his outlook towards all *fliegers*. I confess to a certain amount of apprehension, but in a few moments the woman appeared, and after she had persuaded the belligerent man to withdraw, peace was soon restored.

The next incident was the entrance of a tall, fair youth dressed in the uniform of the *Volkssturm* or Home Guard, followed by no less welcome a person than Arthur, the engineer. The latter made straight towards me and shook me solemnly by the hand. At the time, this action struck me as being perfectly ridiculous, but could only of course, have been intended to express his natural relief that I was safe, and that we were at least temporarily assured of each other's company. We were both longing for a chance to exchange views, but the fair lad, who also spoke good English, insisted that we sat on chairs at opposite ends of the room.

To pass the time as much as anything, I asked the Home Guard if I might go to the lavatory. He took me upstairs and apologised quite graciously for the actions of the man with the revolver. He later appeared with a sandwich of black bread and some kind of tinned meat, which he bade me eat in the lavatory lest anybody in authority should see and disapprove. The food tasted pretty foul, but it was the first I had eaten since the traditional pre-operation breakfast at 9 a.m. that morning and, therefore, did not go down too badly.

When I went downstairs again, the fair youth indicated that it was time to go. After a further superficial search, which forced us to yield our escape maps and emergency rations, we set off in an easterly direction. The lad wheeled a bicycle and acted as our guard, and the rear of the company was brought up by the inevitable bunch of excited youngsters.

Arthur and I again made an attempt at talking to each other, but we were quickly, although politely, repressed, and then our guard started to ask a few questions. They all seemed innocent enough and devoid of any purpose except to satisfy his curiosity, and he was not in the least annoyed when we told him we were not allowed to answer. The query as to the number of our comrades who might be wandering around the neighbourhood was one to which we should very much have liked the answer ourselves, because we were naturally anxious to know if all the boys were safe.

The youth then told us that an aircraft had crashed 8 miles away, and we assumed at the time that we preserved security by showing no concern at this information. It was what we expected, anyway, but as events transpired, the statement had every appearance of a deliberate falsehood. Perhaps our guard was not quite so green as we believed.

Once again, as we marched slowly up the little valley, we were impressed by the beauty and peacefulness of our surroundings. The scene was almost typically English, with the rising land in front of us falling away to a low mountain top, new-born lambs gambolling happily in the fields immediately off the roadside, and the many varieties of trees just bursting into bud. Dusk was falling rapidly and the thought that struck me most was how unreal it all seemed – how can this be war with my pals and I in a comparatively grim situation? Any minute now I am bound to wake up and find myself back in my old bed in the Nissen hut at base!

After walking for about half an hour we came to the somewhat larger village of Schmallenberg, and were led into what definitely appeared to be a farmhouse. We were put into a room that from its slightly official appearance might have been somebody's headquarters. Men, women and children kept coming in and out, talking loudly and of course, to us, quite unintelligibly; the telephone rang frequently and everything seemed to point to the fact that frantic endeavours were being made to cope with a situation as unique as it was unexpected in this backwater of the Reich.

In a little while our fair-haired guard bade us a polite good evening and took his departure. As nobody seemed to have a great deal of concern for us any more, Arthur and I were at last able to talk to each other. I told him my story, and learnt from him that he thought he must have been second out of the aircraft. He had landed flat on his back with a bump that had knocked every breath out of his body. Although he had quickly struggled to his feet and made for the nearest cover, he had been badly short of wind, and had been caught by a civilian with a revolver before he had gone 200 yards. Of the others, like me, he knew nothing at all.

By about 8 p.m. the crowd had subsided somewhat, until finally only two men were left, who, it transpired, were to take turns at guarding us for the night. There was a wood-burning fire at one end of the room and we were invited to sit by it, which we did, grateful for every consideration these people cared to show us. It was not long before a further outburst of chatter on the other side of the door, terminated with the entrance of Jack, our Australian rear-gunner, carrying his own chute and harness and looking as bright and cheerful as ever. He drew a chair to the fire, and as there seemed no further objection to our conversing among ourselves, we listened with great eagerness to his side of the story.

Jack, like myself, had come down practically in the middle of a village, and had been captured immediately. He had, however, been taken before some fairly high officers of the German Army, and had been subjected to some considerable interrogation. He was rather given to the opinion that he had seen five other parachutes in the air, but he was not sure of this. In any case, it did not help a lot in deciding whether all seven had got out, because Jack, departing all on his own from the rear turret, would have no idea as to the order of his exit. The only man who could be certain that six besides himself had baled out would be the skipper, whose duty would be to remain until all had gone, and unfortunately he was not here to tell the tale.

As the evening wore on, it looked as though three was going to be our maximum muster, and so it proved to be. I started to wonder how long we should be fated to be companions in misfortune. Arthur, or Sergeant Biles, to give him his full title, was about 21 years old, unmarried, and with a war that had been going on since he was 15, he had seen little of life to interest him except in his Royal Air Force service. As a consequence, he and I (at 33) had little in common, except that we were both non-smokers and practically non-drinkers, and had not been given to going out much together back at dear old base.

Pilot Officer Jack Acheson, on the other hand, was as bright and breezy a person as one could wish to meet anywhere. His one vice, in my opinion, was a tendency to exaggerate and to be erratic in his opinions. Thus, one minute he would be on one side of the fence, and the next moment would be arguing hotly in favour of the other party! He was about 23, and married with his wife and small daughter, whom he had never seen, back in Australia. For all his faults, he was jolly good company, although as in Arthur's case he and I had not knocked around a great deal together.

I must have fallen asleep whilst thus musing, for I awoke to hear a considerable altercation going on in German. For the second time I was treated to an example of the uncertainty of the German temper. Jack was smoking his pipe, which, he assured us, had actually been lit for him by one of our two guards. The other guard, after storming and shouting at him for fully half a minute, finally stepped forward snatched the pipe from Jack's mouth and smashed it in two on the table. As Jack said, you have to be careful with these brutes, but why didn't the fellow say he didn't want him to smoke!

We didn't fancy this fellow at all, and felt quite relieved when the other one took over. With a whispered indication not to tell anybody, he also brought us all a slice of bread and treacle. Jack and Arthur did not seem much inclined to eat their portions, despite my warnings that we did not know when we might get any more. I was quite grieved to see some of the 'meal' going on the fire (though that was better than leaving it lying around). Indeed, it did turn out to be better fare than we were to get for some considerable time.

There was a crude sofa by the side of the table and whilst we had not liked to get on this uninvited, our guard who was an old man, with a rather kindly face, indicated that we might use it. Jack and I sat down and tried to get some sleep with our heads rested on the table. Arthur, stretching his massive bulk onto all three chairs placed in a row, was soon snoring loudly. I only dozed fitfully, and during one of my wakeful periods I noticed that the old guard was fast asleep; I was tempted to wake the others and suggest that we make a bolt for it. I have little doubt that we could have got out of the house, but as I viewed it we were all tired, hungry and dispirited. We had neither maps nor rations, and, above all, the length of start we should get was problematical, being dependent on how long the old man would sleep after we had gone. I told the others about it in the morning, and they agreed with me. However, we wondered, as we did many times afterwards, whether most of the folk who had charge of us would have been jolly glad to learn that we had disappeared – and no questions asked!

Dawn came at last, much earlier, or so it seemed to us, than it did in England. Perhaps that was because we had not been getting up very early of late, and so had not kept abreast of the rapid lengthening of the days. The guard drew the curtains and opened the window wide, an action which, once again, seemed to be very deliberate. He went out of the room, and we could see out into the street, which was on the same level and practically deserted. It was awfully tempting, but we did not want to get a bullet in the back at that stage of the war, and so with difficulty we kept our seats.

The same impressions returned when I went upstairs to the toilet. The previous night someone had come with us and stood outside, but this morning we seemed to be allowed to wander up at will, and I personally spent quite a long time surveying the immediate landscape. The lavatory window was quite easy to get through, with a reasonable drop of some 12 feet on to soft ground, and about half a mile away over a mist-soaked valley was an inviting-looking wood. I think that if it had not meant letting the other lads down, I should have dropped out of that window there and then. But once again it was a matter for pure conjecture as to how far I should have got before my absence was discovered.

I rejoined my comrades in due course, and we were treated to a slice of black bread and margarine with a cup of black coffee for our breakfast. We began to think that we were going to see a mighty lot of this black bread during our stay in the Reich, a line of reasoning that was to prove accurate! Soon afterwards our guard, the kind-faced one, brought in a large accumulation of tangled up parachutes, harnesses and 'Mae Wests' and ordered us to sort them out. I cannot remember how many of each were there, but despite the pile I doubt if the full equipment of all three of us was covered. Then he wheeled in an outsize bicycle, with immense balloon tyres (we hadn't realised it until then, but all the German bicycles seemed to have colossal tyres, nearly as big as our motorcycle tyres, and it struck us that they must have been very comfortable to ride, but hard to push). Following his gesticulated orders, we loaded all the stuff on top of the machine, tied it on with a few odd bits of string, and trundled the contrivance out of the house and along the road to a destination that we learnt was Fredeberg, 6 kilometres away.

A kilometre is roughly five-eighths of a mile, and as the mathematician of the party I was soon able to manipulate the conversion without any special mental effort. This journey looked like being about 4 miles, which we considered to be plenty far enough on the breakfast we had eaten, and with our burden as it was. After walking a few minutes, we stopped at a wayside farm and a further issue of parachutes etc. was dumped on us. Here, I noticed with a little thrill that Ron's harness was among the gear. Nobody else spotted it because the stuff we had was so jumbled up that we had lost all interest in it, but I had happened to don Ron's harness only the day before by mistake. I had at once discarded it because it was too big for me, but I had noticed the number 250 stamped on the side. There was no doubt in my mind that this was his harness, but the problem for which we had no solution was 'where was Ron?'.

Somehow or other we got this lot on as well, and then took it in turns to rest while one of us held the stuff in place and another one steered the bicycle. We told one or two fair young damsels whom we passed along the road that the parachute silk, which was beginning to trail in the dust, would make them some very nice underwear, but as they didn't understand our remarks, neither they nor our guard suspected that we might be being a trifle indelicate!

Our spirits were brighter this morning and we took the expedition as part of the day's work. There were many things we wanted to discuss, but our guard kept very close. We deemed it wiser not to talk too much, as he might have a knowledge of English, which up to now he had not professed. Another problem that occupied my mind was how to get rid of my Air Ministry watch, which I knew was a valuable piece of booty and which I did not think would remain with me much longer. I was unlucky in this matter, however, because the old man never took his eyes off us, and the immediate vicinity of the roadside did not have any ditches nor water of any kind into which I could dump the article.

At length we arrived at Fredeberg, which proved to be a very pleasant holiday type of town, where people probably came for fishing and shooting holidays. There were any number of pensions (boarding houses) and *gasthofs*, which we assumed with fair reason to be guest houses. There did not appear to have been any enemy activity (it seemed odd how quickly we came to use the term 'enemy aircraft' to describe our own Allied machines), but an air-raid siren sounded with a terrific clatter as we passed through the centre of the town. Simultaneously, a couple of Army officers indicated in no uncertain terms that they would very much like to shoot us! Our guard reasoned with them, however, and without any further show of hostility from the natives we dumped our burden and were led into the office of some high official who would almost surely be the burgomaster.

There was a queue of women outside the office and a couple inside. We were struck by the looks of sadness and suffering on the faces of them all.

Of the nature of their business we had no idea, but the burgomaster was a cruel-looking man, and whatever it was they wanted we had no doubt that it took an awful amount of securing.

In the room also were two German soldiers, to whom our old guard handed us over. Then with a brief nod to us, he disappeared. We didn't much care for the look of these men either, and they proceeded to search us thoroughly and without any ceremony. Everything we had of value and otherwise was taken from us, and whilst protest seemed useless, we were to learn later that we should have been given a receipt if there was to be any hope of our eventually recovering those articles of a non-military character.

When this performance was at last over, we were led out of the building, back up the road down which we had come, and eventually our guards stopped outside a building, which had every appearance of being the local prison. As the door was opened, our worst fears were confirmed, because the smell and general aspect of the place reminded us vividly of the Nazi gaols we had read about at home. A stout inside door was pushed open, we were thrust inside a cold miserable-looking cell amid a pile of dirty straw, and left bewildered to blink around as the cell door clanged shut.

CHAPTER THREE

Out of Gaol

We did not have very long to ruminate on the obvious shortcomings of this apartment, because in less than a minute the soldiers reappeared and more or less pushed us out of this cell and into the one next door. The atmosphere of this cell at once smote us as being as stiflingly hot and stuffy as the other had been cold and dark. We wondered vaguely whether this was the famous hot and cold treatment that we had heard was used to make prisoners talk, but when we found that there was a glass window that could be opened to let in a fair amount of fresh air between stout iron bars, we decided that this was not so. In fact, we soon began to realise that the presence of the small wood-burning fire, which was the cause of all the warmth, was to make all the difference between comparative comfort and sheer misery – provided we were allowed to keep it going.

The cell was about 10 feet long from the window to the door, and about 8 feet wide. Except for a narrow passage down one side and along the end by the door, the whole of the floor space was covered by a dais raised a foot above the ground, which, for want of a more exact term, we called the 'bed'. This article, made of wood, and having a short slope at the end against the wall, was in two sections, each of which could be lifted off the ground. A rapid inspection revealed the presence of a large quantity of logs – enough, we thought, to last a fair sized siege!

When we had cooled off from our walk, and the sun had passed from our window, which it did pretty soon owing to the presence of a large house on the other side of the prison wall, we found that the cell was comfortable, but none too warm. We dragged out a good supply of logs and put them on top of the stove. We considered that, at all costs, the fire would have to be kept going if we were to get any sleep at night. We completed our survey of the cell, finding a small peephole in the door, through which we could get an idea of what went on outside, and a larger hole at the top end of the wall by the door, through which we could see into the cell that we had vacated. However, owing to the thickness of the wall, it was not possible to see what was happening in there. There was an electric light fitted with no bulb, guarded by a small wire grille, and a rack with about six coat hooks, the purpose of which was obscure. As this seemed to complete the entire fixtures and fittings of our apartment, we were able to make a very careful inspection for a possible microphone, and to decide that if we kept our voices down it would be safe to talk. Outside the window we could see a narrow courtyard containing a lot more timber ready for chopping. There was a wall some 12 feet high and at the end on our right a big door the same height, leading to the main street of the town.

We settled ourselves as comfortably on the bed as was possible, using scarves or gloves to soften the 'pillow' that was automatically furnished by the slope against the wall. We began to try and sort out a few of the problems that we had been turning over in our minds since yesterday afternoon.

'I'm afraid I'm dreadfully vague,' I said to Arthur 'as to what it was that made us have to get out in such a fearful hurry after the Skipper gave the order to fix parachutes.'

'If you drove your motor car with no oil in the engine what do you suppose would happen?,' interrupted Jack.

'I don't know, I've never tried it. Something pretty ghastly I expect.'

'Well, there you are,' said Arthur, 'the port inner had reached the stage where it had no oil left in it at all, and this caused the revolutions to get faster and faster, owing to the "windmilling" effect of the propeller in the slipstream.'

'Would she have caught fire, then?'

'Smoke was pouring from her then,' he replied, 'and the old Skip knew that she might burst into flames at any minute.'

'But suppose it had,' I pursued, 'couldn't you have put it out – aren't there some special gadgets for that kind of thing?'

'Yes, but he wasn't able to get it out, and it might have been only a matter of seconds before the whole aircraft was ablaze.'

'Nice thought,' said Jack. Do you remember the case of poor old Johnny D. . . . a few weeks ago? His aircraft was seen to be streaking for the Rhine with an engine on fire. Nobody got out, and before they could reach friendly territory the whole issue burst into flames, and went straight into the deck. Nobody could have had a chance.'

'Looks as though the Skip did us well, taking it all round.' I remarked, 'but it's an awful pity that we don't know where the rest of the boys have got to.'

We carried on talking in monotones for some time, hoping, surmising and trying to form some plausible theories to account for our comrades. Eventually, we were interrupted by a babel of voices in the courtyard. We got up and were greeted at the window by several smiling and friendly faces – there were both men and women, and even some babies. We learnt that there were Russians, French, Poles and Dutch, all apparently prisoners and glad of the opportunity to pass the time of day with us. Not that we could understand much of what was said except from the Frenchmen, but there are times when looks and gestures can say as much as words.

There were two of whom we were going to see a lot during our stay in the prison – one a pleasant-faced Polish girl called Helena, and the other a pretty, sad-eyed Russian lass named Valentina. By a motion to the mouth and the use of the word *'essen'*, which could not mean anything else but 'eat', Helena enquired if we had dined. We shook our heads emphatically to indicate that we had not, neither did we think we stood much chance of so doing. Valentina stayed with us and in a few minutes Helena came back with a billy-can full of hot soup – at least a few strings of carrot floated around like goldfish in a pale sea of yellow liquid, but we realised that is was probably the girls' own rations they were offering and we were thus very grateful. We ate as much as we could of the stuff to satisfy our hunger, which by this time was becoming rather noticeable.

The girls stayed to 'chat' to us for quite a while and we for our part tried to make out how they fitted into the scheme of things in this gloomy gaol. As Jack had remarked (and we thought we detected a change in his tone as he said it) 'it seems to be a mixed clink'. The fact that these two girls were clean and dressed to a far better standard than any of the other prisoners pointed to their being kept there for the only obvious purpose. Valentina showed us how her hands had been burnt by Germans, and that, coupled with the immense sadness in her eyes, told us that she had been no ready victim for the fate that had overtaken her. Poor kids, perhaps at the end of the war they were able to return to the homes whence they must have been snatched when they were but schoolgirls.

After a while the girls disappeared rather hastily, which seemed to indicate that whoever had charge of them had been away and was now back, and we returned to our roost.

Except for the occasional blare of a siren, all was peace and quiet. We tried to weigh the sirens up – there seemed to be three varieties. One was the long straight note like our English 'All clear', another a deep warbling tone which died almost away before coming up again, and the third a fast, warbling sound, which hardly changed in pitch at all. We thought that if the straight note was 'All clear', then one of the other two must be a preliminary warning and the other an 'imminent'. But the theory didn't work, because we were hearing 'imminents' before 'preliminaries' just as often as the other way round! We were to find out much later on that the fast warble was to indicate the approach of fighters and other light aircraft, and the deep warble was reserved for those occasions when heavy bombers were on the prowl – which, we reflected grimly, 'they can be as often as they like provided they steer clear of Fredeberg!'

The afternoon wore on, and there seemed no evidence of our gaolers desiring to visit us. The question of personal convenience was becoming rather pressing, and Arthur, who was experiencing grave discomfort, eventually found beneath the bed a small empty condensed milk tin about a couple of inches in height. The tin had two small holes already pierced in the lid, and the problem was how to get the rest of the lid off so that it could be used as a container. Arthur at last found that one of the staples holding down the grille over the lamp socket was loose. By using this and piercing many more holes in the top of the tin, he at last achieved the desired result. It was then a case of several visits, with a pal to stand by to empty each tinful out of the window, but we enjoyed quite a good laugh. We were not in the least abashed when the courtyard began to fill with prisoners again, and our antics if not actually witnessed must at least have been guessed at. Necessity knows no laws, and we were, at any rate, preserving a certain amount of hygiene! Our other problem when it arose, was much more expeditiously solved by the use of the tray below the fireplace, followed by the rapid burning of the contents.

About this time quite a few of those outside began to hand us in old and very stale hunks and crusts of black bread, for which, I must admit, we got the impression they had no further use! Still, they meant well, and whilst we didn't feel quite that hungry then, we built up a little store beneath the bed, for there seemed to be no telling whether those who had left us here might have forgotten all about us.

Dusk, like dawn, seemed to arrive earlier than at home (we knew the time from a nearby clock that chimed the quarters as well as the hours). As we had no light the only thing left for us to do was 'to take an early night'. We were scared stiff lest we should sleep too well and let the fire go out, but we need not have worried. For several hours there was a terrific racket going on outside, with the sound of German male voices rising above the shrill howls of at least three young babies – we guessed it must be visiting night! Far into the night those wee babies cried, and there always seemed to be at least one of us awake, so that the fire was kept alight, and we were by no means unappreciative of the kindly thought that had provided it for us.

When we finally got up and stretched ourselves, we were staggered to see how many logs we had used. We had stacked a big pile to dry by the fire, and they had practically all gone. We decided that with a little more care, the remaining stock might be made to last a week.

A considerable commotion outside drew our attention to the fact that a large part of the prison population, including three infants, seemed to be on the point of evacuating. Luggage was being tied up onto carts and there was much excited chatter and gesticulation. After a while, the party left by the big gate, waving us goodbye and leaving us still further supplies of even staler bread. We came to the conclusion that they were probably only passing through the town, and had stopped here for one, or, at the most, two nights. The prison, at any rate was never as noisy afterwards as it had been up to now.

At around 9 a.m. the door to the prison opened at last to admit a German woman of about 35 years of age, with features not unbeautiful but desperately stern. She deposited three mugs of black coffee and three pieces of dry black bread on the bed, put a pail down on the floor and departed without any ceremony. We made the best we could of the meal, and surveyed the pail, which we thought might be a good deal more convenient than our existing arrangements, but was not likely to be as sanitary!

The day was again fine, and apart from the ever-present wail of the sirens, little happened to disturb our peace. Valentina and Helena came to the window during the morning and we were quite pleased to see them and exchange a few more views in our language of signs and gestures. A finely built Dutchman, whose name we learnt was Jan, also got quite friendly with us, but the visits of all three were brief, and there was little for us to do apart from stoking the fire and gazing out of the window. Inevitably we spent a fair amount of time studying the bars to the window, but they looked pretty solid, although there was some evidence that the middle one had been got out at some time and subsequently restored.

We slept a bit, and talked a bit, and eventually around noon our wardress brought in a can each of potato soup, which actually tasted quite wholesome. We considered that things were looking up and perhaps we were even going to be fed three meals a day, but we took no chances and saved a little of our soup, which we kept warm by placing the cans on top of the fireplace.

During one of our chats to the girls later that afternoon, we indicated that we thought that if we had an axe we might possibly be able to hack away the concrete around two of the bars, and thus get away during the night. It gave us an immense surprise, though, when Valentina slipped away and returned in a few moments with an extremely useful-looking chopper, which she handed through the bars. At the same time, she made it understood that she would be able to get civilian clothes.

We wondered if and when we dared risk the noise that the tool would undoubtedly create, but we started a little tentative chipping just to see. We had not made much impression when Jan appeared and claimed what seemed to be his axe, and whilst we thought our hopes of escape were going to be dashed, such was not the case. Jan indicated, and it was truly amazing how much conversation we managed to carry on without speaking a word of each other's language, that he would like to come with us. When we told him, by means of a crude sketch, that the Allies had a bridgehead over the Rhine at Remagen, he was wildly elated. The information had obviously not been allowed to get into the prison. His idea seemed to be that tomorrow, which would be Sunday, the wardress would be out all afternoon. He seemed to think it would not take him long to hack away the bars from the outside, as long as he could carry on uninterrupted. The bars would be left loose until after dark and then, he told us, one man over the gate could unbolt it from the outside, and let the others through.

We ourselves were not unexcited, for we had seen enough of the prison system and its occupants to know that we were the only ones who were at all well guarded.

There was nothing else we could do that day, however, and so we settled down to our early bed once more. That night, we were disturbed by the arrival of supper. We found that the German woman had sploshed a ghastly-looking mixture on top of our saved soup, which we thought might contain a bit of meat, but which turned out to be almost entirely bread. The whole lot stirred up was horrible, and we all went to bed practically supperless.

Sunday dawned, bright and fine once more, and breakfast was repeated as on the day before. We indicated that our pail needed emptying. I was detailed for the job, and from what I saw of the prison sanitary arrangements outside, I decided that the pail system was not so bad after all. But

I shuddered to think what it would have been like in the summer, when the flies started to buzz around. We got quite a surprise when we made signs that we would like a wash, our first since Thursday morning back at base. Not only was our request granted, but little Helena brought us her own soap and towel. She also provided a mirror, and with three days' growth of beard I looked a fearsome sight, but I can't say that the fact bothered me much! I was always cursed with a strong growth, and by comparison the hair on the faces of the other two did not look too bad.

Once again, it was a morning of sirens, solitude and slumber. I never seemed to feel as sleepy as my comrades and it would take a whole book on its own to recount the thoughts that used to follow one another through my brain in these periods of forced inactivity. First and foremost, I would try to picture the scene at home where my wife with a boy and a girl of school age, had just presented me with a further son. Up to now I had been luckier than a good many, for I had had regular leave, my children had not grown up without my seeing something of them, and I had actually been pretty near at hand when the third was born.

The morning following the day of disaster my wife would get a telegram from official sources, which would just make the bald announcement that I was missing on active service. It might have been received an hour or two after my last letter to her, which I had given a friend to post just before take-off on the fateful day. With now what seemed exquisite irony, I had told her to keep her fingers tightly crossed for me, as the last half dozen trips often proved the most hazardous. Yet for all the mental strain, I knew she would keep the flag flying. My one big hope was that the shock would not affect her feeding of the latest arrival.

We did not see any of our friends again until after the midday allocation of soup, but then Jan came around and reaffirmed his plans for our escape. It would be a wonderful feat if we could make it. From my pretty accurate knowledge of the spot where we baled out, I calculated that we would have to travel no more than 50 miles in a straight line to make contact with our forces at the spot where they were last Thursday, and they might have pushed in a good deal further since then. We didn't know enough of the country over which we should have to travel to realise that the 50 miles would become a full hundred, but experience was to show. . . .

Around 2 p.m. the prison became very quiet and deserted, and it suddenly occurred to us that there was a hitch in the plans somewhere. We made contact with Jan through the peephole in the cell door. After a great deal of puzzling, it was brought home to us that the door leading out into the courtyard was locked and nobody could get out of doors. Suddenly, from the adjoining cell there came bursts of songs and laughter, which persisted for so long that I was prompted to suggest to Arthur that I should stand on his shoulder and have a look through the hole in the wall to see if I could find out what was going on. I sang a tune myself into the cavity, and in a few moments Valentina's smiling face was looking through at me, obviously enjoying the diversion!

It was all very touching, but I was certain that whenever the vocalists next door paused for breath, I could hear the steady rasping sound of a file against metal. Jack, with his eye glued to the peephole, reported that Jan had been out two or three times and appeared to be making an inspection of our door, as though he was thinking up a way of opening it. Could the plan now be revised so that Jan would be able to get us out of our cell and into the other one, the bars of whose window were already as good as fixed? Or was the Dutchman really no longer interested in us now that he had got an idea of where to make for, and had been foiled in his attempt to remove our bars? We couldn't make it out, or we just daren't hope for too much.

We expected even less when at supper time the wardress brought with her one of the two soldiers who had led us into this place. She indicated, with the first smile we had seen on her undoubtedly comely face, that we were moving out at 5 a.m., and of all the places in Germany, we were going to Arnsberg, our very target of the previous Thursday! From what we could gather, we were going to join English and American comrades. Whilst we still hoped than Jan might do his stuff, we reflected that if he didn't, we ought, at least, to be somewhere a little more civilised. There would also be a chance of meeting the Skipper and the rest of the boys.

We went to bed once more, I with the silent prayer that I always uttered for the safety of us all and the peace of mind of those at home. If Jan was going to free us, we reckoned that he ought not to leave it until later than midnight. We wondered grimly if he knew that 5 a.m. was zero hour.

We slung the logs on the fire recklessly that night and made the room so hot that we all awoke around 3 a.m. and lay waiting for the next chime of the hour so as to see whether any hope remained. Apparently none did, and at 5 a.m., prompt to the minute, the same two soldiers appeared. We were led, baffled and bewildered, into the cool stillness of a morning that promised yet another brilliant day to follow.

CHAPTER FOUR

Hitch-hiking

We were to travel, it seemed, by train. We already knew where the railway station, or *bahnhof*, was, because we had noticed the approach to it, just beyond the burgomaster's office. In the days that followed, the word *'bahnhof'* was to be constantly on our lips. We certainly had no idea then that the one at Fredeberg was to be among the very few that we saw that was untouched by the action of Allied aircraft.

It was a very handsome railway station, and a very big improvement on its prototype in England. Here was no cold, dark and gloomy general waiting room with the inevitable hard horsehair seats and empty fireplace, but a brightly lit prosperous-looking apartment. It was centrally heated, with an attractive refreshment bar at one end, which actually opened up at 6 a.m., although it did not appear to have a lot to sell. Everything was beautifully clean, and there were neat glass-topped tables all around, each with its quota of four modern chairs – the kind that give you the impression that you are going to fall off them, although you never do, of course. I think that if all the subsequent *bahnhofs* that we saw, smashed to little pieces, had been anything like this one, then it was a very great pity that it had to be done. It would have been more fitting had a similar fate befallen some of our own stations, so that some inspired individual could have been detailed to rebuild them on the German pattern.

We were allowed to sit down in the waiting room, in which there were only a handful of people, mostly quite pleasant-looking civilians. Some, quite ignorant of our identity, tried to pass the time of day with us, but were quickly stopped by our guards. The two soldiers had been reinforced by two civilians whom we took to be members of the *Volkssturm*. We correctly surmised that the soldiers only intended to hang around a little, perhaps to check the train in, before handing us over to the Home Guards.

After a wait of about half and hour, a train pulled in, which soon proved not to be ours. It disgorged a fairly large crowd into the waiting room, thus causing us to have to yield our seats. It was obvious that long waits were customary, for with no show of haste, everybody began to pull out food and drink. They then began their breakfasts in a manner that showed that they were well practised in not relying on local supplies of food. One of the members of the *Volkssturm* offered us each half a meat sandwich, which tasted very nice. We thought this was quite kind of him, as it was obviously from his own rations.

After we had been in the room for about three hours, somebody came in and shouted out a message, which seemed to convey that there would be no more trains today. (We were to discover later that few, if any, trains ran in the daytime in that part of Germany, and we have since wondered why these people were apparently more optimistic than the many would-be travellers we met afterwards.) This was the signal for everybody to pack up their food and belongings and leave the station. With some gloom we followed our guards out into the road. Within five minutes we were sitting on our old bed in the little cell, concerned only with one important factor – was the fire still lit?

We hardly had time to begin to kindle the last glowing embers before the two civilians came back again. They hurried us out into the street, muttering something about *autobus*, which sounded to us as if we might be going to travel by road. We were more or less chased at the double towards the market square, where a covered wagon was drawn up, and seemed to be waiting to get us on board before pulling out. We were bundled inside, finding about ten other passengers already installed. We were left to make ourselves as comfortable as possible amid a pile of empty flour sacks and a large quantity of assorted articles of hardware.

Our fellow passengers were a mixed crowd, and included old women, some of them obviously gentlefolk, as well as a baby in arms. In England, this mode of travel would be called 'hitch-hiking', and had considerable popularity among members of the forces going on short leave. However, then, it would be exceptional to find it indulged in by ordinary people in civilian clothes. Over in Germany, we found, it was just about the only way left to travel in the daytime, and quite a good stage of organisation had been reached. At every busy road intersection, in or out of the towns, would be standing a member of the police force, who would wave to a halt practically everything on wheels, motorcycles included. The driver would have to give details of his route, and invariably about twice as many people as the vehicle could comfortably hold would be packed inside. Invariably, a man would be perched in a precarious position outside, in the case of cars on the right-hand side front mudguard, whose sole job was to give an immediate warning to the driver of the approach of enemy aircraft.

We had our first illustration that morning of how a journey to nearly anywhere by road or rail would prove to be about twice as long as the actual distance measured in a straight line on the map. My place on the truck did not give me a very good view of the signposts, but I gathered that our route to Arnsberg lay through the town of Lenne and then all along the valley to the Lenne river, to a point where a road branched off to the right through Stockum and Sundern. At any rate, the journey of about 25 miles as the crow would fly took us all morning, and our guard said that the distance was around 70 kilometres.

We spent by no means all the time in the wagon, because it seemed to be completely lacking in power. At even the smallest hill, it was necessary for all the men to get out and assist to push it to the top. We also stopped several times to deliver items of hardware, and altogether I suppose the trip was made a good deal more interesting than a similar one by the more orthodox English road coach would have been. At long length just before noon, we reached our destination, and bundled ourselves into the street to await further developments.

These came a good deal more quickly than we anticipated, and in a form that was totally unexpected. We had thought that the town seemed rather quiet, and casually assumed that there might be an air-raid warning on; we had overlooked the fact that since last Thursday, at any rate, a siren round these parts would be regarded as more than a mere formality. We looked up on hearing the distant drone of multi-engined aircraft, and saw a neat squadron of Lancasters sailing along majestically. With no thought of any immediate danger, we paused for a few seconds to admire the formation.

'Can't be our mob,' observed Jack with some sarcasm, 'the formation's far too good!'

'Good heavens, look at that!' I cried the next second. They looked and saw what I had seen, a beautiful cluster of what subsequently proved to be a mixture of the massive $5^1/_2$-ton and the new 10-ton bombs, proceeding earthwards in a manner fascinating to watch, but far too rapid to be healthy.

We got into the prone position immediately, whilst our guards, fresh from the unbombed Fredeberg, and in any case having no idea of the immense lethal power of these earthquake-producing bombs, merely stood and watched. A report of that raid stated that one house was lifted bodily and deposited 30 miles away, in which case it was probable that in our position (approximately a mile from the point of impact) we were too far away to get any of the immediate effects, and too near to suffer any harm from the showers of debris that passed overhead.

At any rate, the whole experience shook us considerably, and I think we can claim it to be unique. These big bombs, which accounted for such RAF triumphs as the breaching of the Moehne dam, and the sinking of the battleship *Tirpitz*, had only been employed for limited and very special targets. To be practically underneath a whole shower of them going down together, and at the very target that we had ourselves been so recently employed, must surely be a unique experience.

The excitement over, we walked on, our guards, no doubt, still wondering what we had made all the fuss about. After about a mile we came up to what certainly appeared to be an authentic prison camp, with any amount of barbed wire and German uniforms floating around. However, it was pleasantly situated on the side of a well-wooded hill, and not at all an unsavoury-looking place in which to pass the remainder of the war.

We were led inside, and after some considerable discussion our guards departed. We were ordered to line up on a pathway overlooking a flight of stone steps, which led down to what was undoubtedly an air-raid shelter.

'There's no sign of any prisoners.' I remarked, 'maybe they're all in the shelter waiting for the all clear.'

'I expect we'll have to live down there,' said Jack gloomily. 'Anyway, the place looks more like a rest camp to me, notice how half of the chaps have a limp or something.'

It certainly did look a bit strange, and as the minutes grew to an hour, and still we stood, we wondered what the devil all these German fellows were doing. They were spending all their time either going up and down the steps, or hanging around never very far from them. Most of those visible were officers, some of them quite high ranking. When an occasional private popped his head up to the top of the steps, he was sent back again in such certain terms, that we became convinced that the whole population of the camp was merely waiting for the all clear. There wasn't an aircraft of any sort in the sky, and to us from England, where shelters were only used as the bombs were actually falling, it seemed a trifle absurd and chicken-hearted. We were to decide in the days to come that we judged these chaps somewhat harshly, for we had not yet had the opportunity of seeing at first hand the devastating effect of the Allied bombing.

Unfortunately, we did not stay to see the end of this little comedy, for with German officers still going up and down the steps, we were placed in the charge of two soldiers, who were given a paper. Without wasting any further time, they led us out of the camp, down the hillside, and back into to centre of Arnsberg. One of these new guards had a bullet hole in the side of his cheek, which he said had been done at Köln (Cologne). We were rather inclined to confirm Jack's impression that the place we had just left was some kind of rest camp, and did not contain any Allied prisoners at all.

When we reached the centre of the town, I tried to convey to our guards, on behalf of our party, that I thought it was time for *essen*. We had received nothing officially since supper time the night before, and the small amount of walking we had done after the three days in gaol, had made us all feel quite weak. I think they understood, but if they had any food they were disinclined to part with it, and there was nothing for us to do but to remain both very hungry and more than a little thirsty.

The policeman at the crossroads did his stuff, and we boarded a covered truck going as far as the town of Neheim. This conveyance was packed to suffocation with passengers of all descriptions, all standing up so as to make more room. Everyone above about $5^1/_2$ feet 6 inches tall had his head bent over to prevent it banging into the canvas cover. It was a nightmare of a ride, and when eventually we reached the town all three of us felt so tired that we were forced to sit down on the pavement whilst awaiting further instructions.

It seemed we were only going as far as Werl, about another 20 kilometres. However, at Neheim a lift proved so difficult to secure, that at length our guards, in despair, ordered us to jump on to a passing horse-drawn dray. Although only going at walking speed, at least it was proceeding in the right direction. This mode of transport proved quite cooling and refreshing, and we were able to enjoy an excellent view of the railway station and yards that had received full and quite recent attention from our comrades. It was a fascinating and yet at the same time quite terrifying sight to see the row upon row of burnt and shattered trucks and coaches. The once handsome station buildings were reduced to mere piles of rubble. The spectacle was one that was soon to become all too familiar and I personally reached the stage, before I left Germany, of becoming tired of gazing on the destruction on the scale that Allied bombing had wrought.

We also received, as we left this pleasant little town of Neheim, many baleful looks from civilians. Some shook their fists at us, giving us every impression that it was only the presence of our soldier guards that saved us from getting more than a little hurt. We were destined to learn on the morrow a good deal more of the dangers attaching to this particular aspect of our situation.

The dray only took us about a mile along the road, before our guards abandoned it in favour of another covered wagon that was coming up behind. It was in this wagon that we had our first experience of the 'air-raid spotter' system in operation. We had only been under way a few minutes before we were ordered, along with the other passengers, to disembark, owing to the presence overhead of the *'flieger'* our 'comrade'. We spent a quite comfortable quarter of an hour in a ditch by the side of a wood. We did not dream for one moment that any of the Thunderbolts would waste valuable time and ammunition on a single truck drawn up by the road side, when there was a prominent railway and station in the town we had just left, which, no doubt, could stand a bit further 'plastering.'

There was an amusing episode when in the distant sky could be seen what looked like a thin spiral of descending smoke. From the shouts of joy and laughter coming from the Germans, we jumped to the same conclusion as they had, that one of the Allied planes had been shot down. It was our turn to laugh (and to give them their due some of the Germans laughed with us) when the 'smoke' drew nearer. As it came right up into view, it devolved itself into a gaggle of geese flying in perfect formation. No doubt, as they looked down on us, they enjoyed the joke as much as we did!

We were in the ditch again three more times during that short run to Werl. On the last occasion, when we were only a couple of kilometres outside the town, our guards ordered us to start walking. Apparently, it was liable to prove at least as quick, if not quicker, than waiting for the wagon to get under way again. We walked right into Werl, receiving a host of ugly looks as we passed through the main street, and about another 3 kilometres out the other side. Eventually, we were led on to an airfield of what, in England, was known as the pre-war type. The administrative buildings and living quarters were built of brick and stone, presenting a totally different appearance to the temporary war-time aerodromes at home, which had little clusters of Nissen or wooden huts usually dispersed among clumps of trees. In fact, the whole layout was so suspiciously reminiscent of English airfields constructed before the war, that we felt that somebody, sometime, must have done a little quiet 'cribbing'. Which side it was we were not prepared to say!

We came to the more or less immediate and unanimous conclusion, that unlike the pleasantly secluded rest camp at Arnsberg, this place, if we were to take it as being our accommodation for the rest of the war, could be considerably improved upon. The number of bomb and blast-shattered buildings that we saw as we passed down the main roadway *en route* to the *Commandant's* office, in no way served to undermine this first impression.

We need not have worried. We had not been standing outside the *Commandant's* office more than half a minute before it became plain to us that, once more, we were far from in the right spot. We heard our guard mumbling something about Russians and Croats. From the amount of subsequent dashing in and out, coupled with excited chatter, we gathered that the prison facilities here were certainly not for the likes of us!

It did not occur to us right at that moment, but it soon became obvious that communications, in this part of the Reich, at any rate, must have become, virtually a thing of the past. How otherwise could those in Fredeberg have been so completely ignorant that Arnsberg, as a POW camp for Allied airmen, no longer existed? (The German wardress, we remembered, had been almost enthusiastic when she dwelt on the chances of our soon being among our comrades.) Similarly, how could the officials in Arnsberg (and there were enough of them) be so unaware that the camp at Werl was devoted to only Russian and Croat slave labour? As we were soon to see, the term POW, as applied to these poor wretches, was merely an unpleasant fiction.

After a few moments hanging around, we were handed over to the care of a huge German corporal, who appeared to own, as his personal bodyguard, a particularly unwholesome and vicious-looking Alsatian dog. I must say, now, that the dog never made any attempt to molest any of us, but then at the same time, we took jolly good care not to give the beast even the semblance of a chance. Civilians, apparently, were subject to even less self discipline than dogs, for as we walked wearily down the main road again, on what we hoped was the last lap for today (it was now around 5 p.m. and we were in sore need of our tea, to say nothing of our dinner and breakfast), a big hulking villain in a blue serge suit came up to us. After hurling a torrent of abuse at nobody in particular, he kicked poor Jack very hard in the seat of his pants. Jack did the right thing in keeping his temper, and making no attempt at retaliation. He told us afterwards that he did not know how he did it. In a few seconds, the corporal had the situation in hand and the man had been sent about his business. I, for may part, was scared out of my wits that it was going to be my turn next!

Our new guard led us down a flight of stone steps into an underground prison that was simply seething with half-naked Russians. Some recognised our uniforms, and greeted us with friendly smiles. There hardly seemed an inch of room in any of the cells that we passed, each of which was no bigger than the one at Fredeberg, and yet must have contained at least twenty of the poor devils. We had become a little inured to hardship in the past four days, but it came as a big relief when we were taken into the very end cell. As the iron door clanged behind us, it appeared that we stood a very good chance of having it to ourselves.

CHAPTER FIVE

The Prison at Werl

We were left alone for about half an hour, which gave us ample time to take stock of our new quarters. The cell was slightly longer and not quite so wide as the one we had left that morning (how much longer than a mere twelve hours ago it seemed). Practically the entire floor space apart from a narrow passage down the centre was occupied by four bunk beds, providing sleeping accommodation for no fewer than eight unfortunate prisoners. The window was much smaller and higher up, and whilst we could just about see out, at a stretch, it was nothing like as convenient as the one at Fredeberg, especially when it came to having a conversation with anybody outside. The iron bars were practically inaccessible from inside the cell, and there was thus little point in spending time in studying them to the extent we had done in our first prison.

An inspection of the beds revealed that only one of them boasted a straw mattress in addition to the hard wooden plank that formed the base. Jack, who many times in the days to come proved his ability to sleep on anything, volunteered to sleep on the boards, and I pointed out to Arthur that with a bit of a squash two of us could share the straw bedding. We had more or less agreed upon this distribution, and resigned ourselves to the fact that we were, in any case, going to be infernally cold (there was a little iron fireplace but it was not connected to any chimney, and was quite patently a dead loss) when our corporal guard, still accompanied by his faithful hound, reappeared.

'*Ein Man*' he barked with a quick gesture of impatience (we soon decided that his bark was a good deal worse than his bite) and our sketchy knowledge of German brought us to the conclusion that one of us was required to go somewhere. The corporal didn't give us any time to decide who should go, but at once grabbed Arthur and led him away. Jack and I were left to meditate as to what fate worse than death might be in store for the poor lad, and for us too, for that matter!

We did not have to worry very long, for corporal, dog and '*ein Man*' were soon back. Arthur carried what looked quite promisingly like *essen* in the shape of a big white tureen full of a porridge-like mixture, and an enormous metal jug of black coffee. From the outer regions our guard, with Arthur's help, quickly produced a small wooden table, a couple of stools and three plates, mugs and spoons. I remarked to the others that there seemed to be every chance that we might be going to enjoy a hot sit-down meal for the first time for nearly five days. Whilst not exactly desirous of mixing the subject with that of food, we realised the necessity of catching our man whilst we had him, and tried him with the single word 'latrine'. He brought us in a canister arrangement not unlike an English milk churn. It was superior to the Fredeberg effort in that it did have a heavy lid to it. Encouraged, we pointed to *'ein* mattress' and indicated that two more would be useful, but in reply the man uttered the single word *'essen'*, and dog at heels, departed.

'Maybe he'll fix it after tea,' I said hopefully, 'come on let's pile in!'

And so we 'piled in'. The contents of the tureen seemed to be barley, and whilst it was sweetened with what would almost surely be saccharin, the taste was rather sickly. Moreover, by this time, the food was nearly cold. The hot coffee was quite welcome, and served to warm us up a bit, but there was a terrific quantity. When we had each drank two cups, there was enough left in the jug to provide drink 'for half the *Luftwaffe'*!

'If we had a razor,' said Jack facetiously, 'we could shave in this – if we had a shaving brush!'

We had barely finished eating when the corporal returned, once more with his bellowed demand for *'ein Man'*. It seemed that he wanted Arthur to wash up, under a tap just outside the door. In fact, whenever he called for '*ein Man*' afterwards, it was Arthur who was the one required. I think this must have been because he knew Jack and I were officers, and in the *Luftwaffe* they seemed to make a very big social distinction between their commissioned and other ranks.

Anyway, Arthur was left to wash up, and Jack and I were led away out of the prison, and down into another 100 yards away. This, again, was packed with with poor hot, unhappy-looking Russians. Our guard gave an order that sent two of them away to return with two straw mattresses and three dirty threadbare blankets. It was by no means without compunction that we realised that it was necessary to rob these unfortunate slaves in order to secure our bedding. However, we reflected, that even if we had wanted to, it would not have been very wise to have refused.

We carted the stuff back to our cell, Arthur brought in the clean eating utensils, and we were left to settle down for the night. It was growing dusk, and appreciably colder. It was obvious that after the nights in the almost too hot cell back at Fredeberg, we were going to experience uncommon difficulty in securing some measure of warmth for our long-suffering bodies. We had yet to experience to the full, the very great difference in the day- and night-time temperatures on the continent, especially during a prolonged spell of fine weather such as this. If we had known what we knew afterwards about German climatic conditions, I suppose we should have been even more apprehensive.

However, we settled down. Jack was soon snoring peacefully, but both Arthur and I are prepared to swear that we were so cold that we never slept a wink! We must have dozed off a little, I suppose, or otherwise the night would have seemed longer than it did, but in any event it appeared plenty long enough. It was a big relief when dawn, at last, showed its first grey threads through the tiny window. Not that there was anything for us to do then, or any method of getting warm, for there was not even the business of stoking the fire, that we had had to attend to before.

It was a different guard that looked in on us at what seemed to be around 8 a.m. that morning. (We could see a clock on a distant building, but the view of the figures seven up to eleven was blocked by an intervening chimney and so our telling of the time was subject to some limitations.) All he did was to stick his head around the door and withdraw. Our next visitors were three or four Russians, who came to see us for a few moments several times afterwards, but although we were naturally very curious, we never did find out how they got in. It is possible that when he was around outside, the guard merely hooked the padlock into the hasp in a manner that rendered it impossible to open the door from inside, although anyone could get in easily from without. The Russians, on the other hand, may have got themselves fixed up with a master key – slaves though they undoubtedly were, they never struck us as being without brains. Any little things they could organise for their own benefit or to the discomfiture of their enemies, they always appeared to have well in hand.

I accepted from one of them the offer of a piece of raw potato, which I thought might assist in cleansing my teeth, about which I was beginning to get a little worried. We also got fixed up with an old razor, which bent and twisted though it was, provided all of us with more than one shave in the days to come. By then, though, I was long past caring about the uncouth appearance that my five days' growth must have presented. One particularly friendly Russian who spoke a little English, then handed us a pack of German cards. We had just settled down to one of our old favourite games back in the Mess at home (modified somewhat because there were only thirty-two cards in the pack), when the door opened once more to admit several German officers – and Diffy.

Poor Diffy – I was the first to spot him, as I was sitting facing the door. I whispered excitedly to the others 'an American!'

The Germans soon left him, and although he wasn't able to tell us much then, it must have been a tremendous relief for him to hear once more friendly English-speaking voices. The poor chap had been beaten up to a terrible extent – his left arm was in a sling, and his other one was bandaged, as were his nose, part of his face and the top of his head. He was obviously in far too bad a way to talk then, but we did learn that the damage had been done by civilians. We made him as comfortable as we could on one of the beds, using all three of the blankets to give him as much warmth as possible.

After that, we did not have a lot more enthusiasm for our cards. The American dozed, the time passing very slowly while we waited for him to wake up so that we might hear his story. At length he sat up, we introduced ourselves and he told us that his parents were of German extraction, so that he was blessed with a quite unpronounceable German-sounding name which boiled down very nicely to 'Diffy'. He was a captain in the US Air Corps, the equivalent to our flight lieutenant, and had been the pilot of a P47, or Thunderbolt, attacking a target not very far from here. Funnily enough, like ourselves, he had not been forced to bale out by any action of the enemy. His single engine had apparently 'packed up' without any warning.

He had come down in what he thought was the important railway town of Soest about ten miles east of Werl, and had at once been set upon by civilians armed with sticks and spades. He had been kicked and harried down the entire length of one street. He had taken the whole beating without attempt at retaliation, which definitely was the only thing to do if he wished to live to tell the tale. Eventually, he had been rescued by some soldiers, and had been taken to a doctor to be patched up in what looked to be an extraordinarily unskilful manner. Diffy thought that his nose was definitely broken, and his hand too, although he was not sure about that. To our minds there seemed little doubt that he ought to be in hospital.

When he had finished his story, the captain sank back wearily on to the bed and asked if we ever got anything to eat round these parts. This gave us the chance to tell him briefly of our own adventures to date, and to explain that the feeding over the past two days had been, to say the least, a little irregular.

It must have been around 3 p.m. before our boredom was relieved at last by the appearance of the Alsatian dog, followed by his lanky master. He seemed rather surprised to learn that we had not eaten, and this time he detailed me to go with Arthur to fetch the food. The meal was similar to that of the night before, with the addition of a hunk of black bread and margarine. Poor old Diffy, despite his obvious hunger, was not able to eat very much. We had our fill but there was still a good deal over, which the corporal, when he returned, handed over to the Russians. The eager greed with which these poor fellows ate up our remains told its own story of hunger and deprivation.

Shortly after this, we were all led out of the prison and taken up for an interview with the *Commandant*. We actually only saw an officer who would be the equivalent of our English adjutant. The entire proceedings seemed to be a formality, because what questions he asked us, in broken English, were not answerable, and he gave us the impression that he did not care whether we answered them or not.

As soon as we got back to the cell, the corporal indicated that it was time for tea, thus proving to Diffy our statement about the irregularity of the meals, for it was only about an hour and a half since we had had dinner. To give this fellow his due, he did seem quite anxious to look after us. It was quite possible that he had issued instructions that we were to be fed during the morning, and that someone had just been careless. He also told us that at 2 a.m. the following day we would be leaving by train for Frankfurt.

The bread and margarine was washed down by a drink of actual tea, prepared by a Russian cook. We were very much surprised, because we had already formed the conclusion that nobody drank anything but coffee in the Fatherland. Whilst Arthur was fetching the tea, Jack and I had been busy collecting an issue of rations for the journey, these consisted of three loaves of bread, about half a pound of margarine and a similar quantity of cheese of the kind that comes in oblong slabs.

'Must be going to be a long trip.' I reflected, little guessing what truth lay behind my words.

About 6 p.m., we had a visitor in the form of a *Luftwaffe* pilot, who said in quite reasonable

English that he had heard we were here, and wanted to have a few words with us. He told us of how he had been a student at Oxford, and how the war, of which he was utterly tired, had interrupted his studies which he was anxious to resume as soon as possible. It was all very touching, and not without interest, but I personally felt convinced from the manner in which he popped in an occasional pert question (such as 'How many were there in your crew?) that he had been sent along to see if we were at all inclined to talk if off our guard.

We took the chance, before he left, of asking if extra bedding could be provided for our American friend. When this had been duly done we finally settled down in the cold once more to snatch what sleep we could ere the bewitching hour of 2 a.m. arrived.

I think I must have slept more soundly that night because it didn't seem anything like as far advanced as 2 a.m. when I awoke to find the room filled with about half a dozen *Luftwaffe* officers, one or two of whom spoke English. We gathered that there was a little celebration going on in their Mess, and that they would be very glad if we could join them for a drink and a chat – not, of course, on military matters! Well, we had been warned about this dodge, too, and after a brief discussion among ourselves, Jack and I said we would be pleased to go along. Arthur, not being an officer, didn't think he ought and Diffy said he was by no means in a fit state to go.

We were led across part of the airfield towards what looked like flying control. We noticed that an armed guard followed at a respectable distance – they were not taking any chances! The Mess proved to be a cosy little room, below ground level. We were given seats, and Cognac and cigars were laid on. It was patent that no effort was spared to make us become aware of what good fellows they thought we were.

We drank their brandy, and very nice it tasted, too, as a change from black coffee. But we insisted from the outset, that we could not possibly deal with questions of a military nature. To be fair, they were not particularly persistent. It was quite possible that if the affair was part of the 'set-up' (and I can see little reason to doubt that it must have been) then those taking part were only acting on the orders of the *Commandant*. It seemed that as long as they could say they had done their job, they were in no way concerned as to its success or otherwise.

We must have stayed in the room for over two hours, because it was nearly 10 p.m. when we reached it, and nearly 1 a.m. when we were led back to our cell. Our hosts drew us into conversation on all manner of innocent subjects, such as sport, music, literature and the like. They all seemed thoroughly good fellows, fed up with the war and anxious to be our firm friends when it was all over. Meanwhile, they couldn't resist the odd little question, which, as in the case of our earlier visitor to the cell, so served to give the game away.

'You came down in the daylight?' said one, who admitted he was an intelligence officer.

As any number of Germans had seen us come down in the daytime, there seemed little point in denying this.

'Well then,' he went on, 'if you came down in the daylight and there were at least four of you in the crew, for you have no pilot here with you, you must have been flying in a Lancaster?'

Politely I pointed out that the question was one that could not be answered. With a shrug, this officer, whom we liked the least of all, gave up the argument.

They all knew that we were going to Frankfurt, and told us that it was a very fine camp, and that we should meet many of our comrades there. We remembered vaguely having been told this before!

At last the party broke up, we were led back to the ignominy of our cell, and crawled on to our beds to snatch the final hour of sleep before it was time to go. I didn't sleep anymore and it seemed an awfully long time before our old corporal came in. He was cursing pretty freely as though something had gone wrong with the arrangements, as indeed did appear to be the case, as it was now after 3 a.m. Hurriedly, we were made to collect our rations, and without further ado, were bundled out into the dim moonlight of the early March morning.

CHAPTER SIX

Karl and Adolf

The morning was bitterly cold, and we all felt very stiff and shivery as we made our way down to the now familiar main roadway towards the gate at which we had entered on Monday evening. There was a sentry on duty at the gate and standing beside him was a little old man in the uniform of the German civil police, who we soon learnt was to act as yet another guard for us.

There was a brief exchange of formalities and then the old man made us fall in in two ranks, and we were marched off down the street. Hardly a word was spoken as we strode along, but I do remember thinking how ridiculously easy it would be to overpower the old man. Without doing anything beyond rendering him ineffective for a few hours, we could have made off into the night. We had the full advantage then, over our other projected escapes, in that we were now equipped with enough food to last several days, but against that was the problem of Diffy's physical condition. The poor chap was obviously in no state to cope with the hardship and strain that must inevitably ensue. It was equally futile to suppose that we could 'fix' our guard and leave Diffy roaming around all night while we made good our departure.

Another good chance of escape therefore had to be turned down. It was not very long before we were back in the town of Werl and had made our way to the railway station. We were taken into the entrance hall, but although there were several people waiting around, the place was in complete and total darkness. The policeman did the only thing possible, and led us outside again. For all he knew we could have wandered off, one at a time in the inky blackness within, and he would have been none the wiser!

Whilst we were standing outside, our guard started to make a little conversation. We discovered that he had a passable knowledge of English, a fact which was to make things easier in the days that we spent in his company. He told us that he was not a Nazi, and that as long as we behaved ourselves, he would look after us (and by this time we were well aware that we should need looking after) and we should be well treated. In response to our enquiry, he told us that the distance to Frankfurt was about 150 miles, and that it would take about two days. We were still innocent enough to wonder how it could possibly take as long as that!

Our walk had warmed us up, but we were beginning to get awfully cold again. As soon as a thin shaft of light coming from under the door indicated that someone at last had organised a bit of illumination within, we were allowed to return indoors. The waiting room had been bombed, we learnt, and we resigned ourselves to what developed into a long and weary wait. We made ourselves as comfortable as possible leaning against the walls or sitting on the floor of the entrance hall. During our wait the party was reinforced by what appeared to be the very much overdue arrival of a second guard, a particularly dirty and uncouth-looking airman.

Dawn was breaking before the train at last drew in, and then our ride only proved to be of about half an hour's duration. To our considerable surprise, we travelled in a westerly direction, as was evidenced by the glow of the dawn behind us. There was hardly a window left in any of the compartments, and as it was a corridor train, the draught was terrible, to say nothing of the temperature, which must have been well below freezing level.

We reached the town of Unna, and although the permanent way had suffered a good bit of bomb damage, we were pleased to see that the *bahnhof* itself appeared to be intact. Moreover, the waiting room into which we were taken was actually warm, and there was room for us to sit down. Many of the passengers had obviously spent the night there, and although we did not know it then, it is likely that some of them were not even passengers. As we learnt later, in most towns a *bahnhof* that was not 'kaput' was just about the only place that anyone passing through could find to rest his bones during the hours of darkness.

We did not wait very long, but as soon as the sun had begun to show its first yellow streaks through the window (it would then be around 6.30 a.m.), we made our way out of the station and up into the centre of the town. We were at once struck by the bustle and activity at this time, which at home we would have described as 'the middle of the night'. When we reached the market square, we found that a policeman with his baton was already quite busy. The crowds waiting for lifts on the street corners were considerable, and being augmented every minute by fresh arrivals.

We took good care not to stray from our guards, for quite a few ugly looks and muttered curses were flung our way. Whether it was because of this or that lifts to where we wanted to go were unobtainable, I do not know, but it was not long before our policeman guard told us that we were going back to the *bahnhof* again.

The crowd in the waiting room had cleared considerably. The bar was now open, although as was the case in Fredeberg, it did not have much in the way of refreshment to dispense. On a signal being given we commenced to make our first meal of bread, margarine and cheese, but we were unduly optimistic in thinking that there might be coffee to wash it down. In fact, we did not even get a drink of water. Still, the food was good and wholesome, although very plain, and I suppose we all enjoyed it, our first repast on a self-supporting basis!

At around 9 a.m. came the inevitable shout, we presumed, 'No more trains today'. This was the signal for the waiting room to empty immediately, and so in a few minutes we found ourselves once again in the market square. 'Things will have to speed up a bit if we are to do it in two days,' I remarked with a much greater hint at the truth than I realised.

About another hour passed before the efforts of the airman to secure a lift were successful. (We were to learn that it was always he who did the negotiating in any matter concerning our travel. We presumed that this was because he appeared to have done the journey before and therefore was acquainted with all the short cuts necessary to get to our particular destination.) By a miracle, we managed to get as far as the town of Iserlohn without any change of transport, although our route lay through the town of Menden, which added about 10 kilometres to the direct distance of 18 kilometres.

Iserlohn is about 20 miles south-east of Dortmund and was the largest in which we had been so far. There was a good deal of evidence of action by our aircraft, and when we left the wagon and walked through the main streets, we were once again the recipients of many sour glances from the civilians. Our guards did their best to hurry us through the busy parts, but there seemed to be frequent halts to enquire the way. We all, especially Diffy, made sure that we did not wander far away from them.

It was during one of these halts that we met a civilian who showed our guards (in what to us appeared to be a defiant manner) a leaflet, obviously dropped from one of our aircraft. It was signed by General Eisenhower and told all members of the German Armed Forces exactly how they should proceed in order to save their lives, by peaceable surrender. The leaflet was printed in both English and German, and it assured the possessor a safe conduct through our lines, if presented to a member of our forces in the proper manner. Altogether, it was a most interesting document and we wondered if the civilian in possession of it was actually a German soldier who intended to take advantage of the scheme at the earliest opportunity.

We left the town, following a road that seemed to go gradually downhill for a long way. Running alongside the route was a single-track electric tramway. Our guards indicated that we might possibly proceed part of the way by tram. However, after waiting a full half hour at a stop, the tram, when it eventually came, was so packed that it seemed impossible to squeeze another living person into it. Nevertheless, quite a few did get on, although it was not to be expected that we should, whilst there were Germans left behind. After seeing the tram leave with its sides almost bulging, we proceeded on foot.

We seemed to walk an awful long way down that hill without getting any nearer to the bottom. As it was our first really long stretch of walking for several days, we wondered how poor old Diffy was coping. We asked him from time to time how he was getting along, but he said that he felt quite alright, although his wounds were obviously giving him a great deal of pain.

There was another ugly incident when at last we reached the bottom of the hill and found a road branching off to the left with a signpost indicating that the distance to Siegen was 100 kilometres. The siren had just sounded and several Thunderbolts were buzzing about overhead, when a group of angry men came rushing up to us armed with sticks, staves and some of them with their revolvers drawn. I am bound to say that the way in which our guards held the situation in hand was admirable. We all felt that if it had not been for them on this and on subsequent occasions, we might have been severely injured, or even lost our lives.

We walked a little further along the road to Siegen and when we were well clear of all the built-up areas, we were told that we could rest in a small wood at the side of the road and partake of our midday meal. Water was obtained from a nearby cottage and served to wash down the bread and cheese that was to become so familiar before the journey was over.

During that stop for lunch, we got to know quite a lot about our guards, with whom we realised it would pay to keep on the best possible terms. The little policeman was called Karl Kremer and he formerly kept a dairy shop in Aachen. He told us that he had no interest whatsoever in the war and that all he really wanted was to get back to his wife and business. We even got as far as suggesting that nobody would be any the wiser if he accomplished this end by the simple means of turning his back for a few moments and letting us disappear into the woods. We had already seen enough of the German system of communications to know that there was not the smallest chance of our being expected by the people in Frankfurt, and as Karl himself explained, if he was taken prisoner by the Allied Forces, he would, as a policeman, merely be sent back to do police duty in his home town.

The whole idea seemed to tempt him somewhat and there were times when we thought he might succumb. However, he told us that if it was found out, he would be shot, and, of course, we did not doubt his word for a moment. The other man, whose name was Adolf, could not speak a single word of English and all we learnt about him was that he had a wife and family in Frankfurt, which explained quite a lot of things that had been puzzling us. How otherwise could such a disreptuable-looking 'erk' have been entrusted with a reasonably responsible job such as this, unless it had been 'wangled' by Karl. We laughed heartily when Karl told us that whilst the journey outwards might take two days, they would spend at least seven on the return trip. We recalled that there might have been times in our service careers when we would have done the same things ourselves, had the opportunity presented itself. We also began to have grave doubts as to whether the two days, which we had at one time thought such a generous allowance, would prove to be anything like enough.

The afternoon wore on and we still lay on the grassy slope, nobody apparently being in the slightest hurry to proceed. Karl did not have any objection to our making ourselves comfortable and snatching a short sleep. Children from the nearby village came and played around us: the view from the wooded slope was exquisite and but for the frequent wail of the sirens and the drone of our own aircraft overhead, we might easily have been lulled into the false impression that we were merely out on a picnic.

At length we pushed on. Siegen, which at one time had been declared our day's objective, was still at least 99 kilometres away. We only walked as far as the nearest railway station, which was less than 5 miles out of Iserlohn and there we waited whilst Adolf made enquiries about trains.

It seemed that there would be one about 6.15 p.m. and as this seemed satisfactory, we all sat down in the waiting room, which at that time was quite warm and sunny.

We pulled out our food once again and I suggested that as it looked like being a good deal more than two days before we reached our destination, it was about time that we introduced some sort of rationing system. Accordingly, we decided that any one meal should not consist of both cheese and margarine in addition to the bread and that the size of the piece of cheese per man should be severely curtailed.

We had been cutting off slices of cheese at least half an inch thick and so we reduced this by half, which, when divided into four, gave us each a piece of cheese per alternate meal, measuring approximately the size of a very small India rubber!

Karl, at this stage, had become so concerned with our welfare, that he even volunteered to go out and buy us some beer. However, although he was gone quite a long time, when he returned he was empty-handed and we were not able to gather the reason why he had not got any. I would say that under the rules governing POWs, the drinking of beer (especially with their guards) would be definitely forbidden.

It grew dark and cold and at about 8 p.m., as the train had still not come, we were taken into the station master's office, where two or three other would-be passengers waited beside a comfortable fire. We were even offered the facility of a wash (our first since Sunday) and, altogether, we felt that the 'proprietor' of this particular station, left no stone unturned to secure our every comfort!

At about 9 p.m., the train puffed slowly into the station and we were bundled into the guard's van, as every inch of sitting and standing room in the coaches seemed to be occupied. The doors would not shut, and our journey, which must have lasted for about two hours, was even colder that the one we had taken that morning. In the van we were sitting on top of some boxes of ammunition destined for Berlin (Heaven only knows how long it would take them to get there by the route they were going). More than once, as we passed through very dark tunnels, we were tempted to pitch the boxes out on to the permanent way, thus satisfying our legitimate rights as POWs, to commit if possible, a little undetected sabotage. I suppose we were deterred chiefly by the fact that the boxes were very hard to shift and in any case would have been missed as soon as we came out of a tunnel, because the moon was very bright and was shining in right through the open doors.

At long last, frozen, aching and weary, we disembarked at the small wayside station at Ohle. Adolf, whom we often admired afterwards for the speed with which he got things organised, led us into a small waiting room in nice time to make ourselves comfortable on the floor before a large proportion of the rest of the passengers discovered that the main waiting room was 'kaput'.

When this waiting room eventually began to fill up, we wondered how many more people would try to get in. As it was, I could never remember seeing so many men, women and children trying to secure rest in such a confined space. Setting aside any question of the smell, it was in some ways a blessing, because with the addition of the fire, we did manage to keep a semblance of warmth, which enabled us to snatch a fitful sleep.

CHAPTER SEVEN

Adolf Takes a Chance

The night seemed long and uncomfortable and when we all awoke for the last time and stretched our legs, we found the fire was out, and that the morning was extremely cold and misty. A brief spell outside the waiting room soon brought us back in again for what warmth it provided; after the fresh air, the aroma inside was quite indescribable. In these circumstances and with as much appetite as we could muster, we broke our fast with the usual bread and margarine, it not being our turn for cheese.

It was now Thursday 22 March and we realised that it was a full week since we had left our base, on the ill-fated expedition. We were still given to occasional reminiscing as to why it had been necessary for us to bale out and whether all the other boys had been comparatively fortunate in their experiences so far, as we had been. Jack, by this time, had reached the stage of being confident that he had seen six other parachutes in the air besides his own, but as has been mentioned before, we were quite accustomed to applying a considerable discount to his figures.

At about 7 p.m., we left the waiting room and boarded a train that Karl said would take us two stations further down the line. It proved to be the same train as on the previous night, and we were pushed into the same draughty guard's van, with the same boxes of ammunition to serve as seats. We reflected hopefully, that if all the ammunition intended for the defence of Berlin was proceeding on its way as rapidly as this lot, then the chances of the city making a long last stand, could not be considered too rosy.

We alighted at Plettenberg, the reason why we could proceed no further being at once obvious: the extreme devastation of the entire station and practically the whole of the nearby permanent way and rolling stock. Once again, anticipating trouble from the civilians, we clung close to Karl and Adolf as we made our way from the station and up into the centre of the town.

Our fears were not unfounded and, it was obvious that we could not spend the time at the side of the road. It was necessary to obtain a lift in the direction in which Adolf said we ought to go. However, this route appeared to lead us back in exactly the direction whence we had come. It was true, as a subsequent study of the map showed, and it became apparent afterwards that a ride of about 15 miles was needed in order to save about 10 miles on the road.

We walked as briskly as possible out of the town and eventually joined the valley of the Lenne in almost exactly the same spot as we had made our turning off to Arnsberg on the previous Monday. We had no idea of this, of course. As a matter of fact, we were quite excited when we saw 'Arnsberg' on the signpost, away to our left, because it meant that we were well west of that town and therefore nearer to our own lines than we had been at any time previously. The possibility of escape was never far from the front of our minds and I could tell that the rest of the boys placed a great deal of faith in me, as navigator, to try and keep something like a mental idea of our position in relation to the situation of our own forces.

We seemed to walk a fairly long distance that morning and although we heard no sirens, there were plenty of enemy aircraft around. We gathered that we must be reaching extremely countrified districts out of earshot of all warnings. The only incident of note occurred when a bad tempered *Luftwaffe* officer indicated in no uncertain manner, that he thought we ought to be shot; I think I can class this as one of the very few incidents in which a member of the Armed Forces appeared to show any disregard for our rights and privileges as POWs.

It was once again a brilliantly fine sunny morning, making as far as we could recollect, about three weeks of fair weather over the whole of the continent. We already knew that the Allied air forces were taking full advantage of this weather. There is not the slightest doubt that had the conditions been any different, the slashing of communications would not have been carried out to the same extent, and the day of our ultimate release might have been put back for weeks, if not months.

As we plodded down the road, we saw a lot of evidence that they expected the war to be coming this way pretty soon, for French POWs were busy in many parts, digging slit trenches and air-raid shelters in the banks at the side of the wood. All these fellows looked at us as we passed, at first suspiciously and then with many evident signs of welcome as they recognised our uniforms. We, for our part, knowing that we should not fraternise with them at all, merely contented ourselves with a brief smile, if we thought our guards were not looking. I did hear one story much later on, of a French POW who had had his head completely bashed in by a Nazi guard, merely because he had smiled at an American POW.

It was well past 1 p.m. when we at length stopped for our midday meal. Our guards selected a pleasant little spot by the side of a cottage, a little way off the main road. Water was supplied in plenty, and the inhabitants of the cottage seemed very friendly and quite anxious to show that they didn't want the war and would be jolly glad when it was over. As was the case yesterday, we were able to indulge in a short nap after we had eaten. Later on, Jack, who had been missing with Karl for quite a time, came back and told us that he had been in the cottage and had been talking for a long time to its occupants. He said that one of their chief everyday pleasures was to listen to the news in German, broadcast from the British Isles.

Once again, nobody appeared to be in any hurry to press on. In the late afternoon, we were invited into the back garden of the cottage and told we could wash if we wished, and even have a shave. Karl very kindly lent me his shaving tackle, which enabled me to manage successfully, although I am afraid that his blade could not have been a lot of good when I had finished.

We had our tea and heard from Karl that it was proposed to spend the night in a 'bus that had run off the road, a few hundred yards back from the cottage'. We thought that this might prove quite comfortable and even if chilly, ought at least to be reasonably clean and wholesome. Everything was proceeding peacefully and calmly until the approach of two officers of the Wehrmacht, who spoke volubly and at some length in a manner that appeared to cause a good deal of concern to our guards.

Whether it was these officers or the fact that disquietening information had come over the 6 p.m. broadcast (or possibly both) we did not know, but it was obvious that something was creating a sudden panic. I surmise now that this could only have been the news that General Patton's Third Army had crossed the Rhine at Koblenz and were pressing on at great speed towards Frankfurt. We could not expect to be told these things of course (although it can be imagined how cheered we would have been), but it does seem to me now that the cause of all the excitement was Adolf's sudden realisation that he was going to have to put on a very big spurt if he was to reach Frankfurt before the American troops.

At any rate, our kit was packed with every evidence of considerable hurry and we were marched away from the cottage at a brisk speed towards a railway station, which Karl said was only 3 kilometres away. Unlike those of the English-speaking guards of the days immediately preceeding our liberation, Karl's estimates of distance usually proved to be pretty accurate. In about half an hour, we reached a station and settled ourselves in an extremely cold waiting room, knowing by this time that the train scheduled for 9 p.m. would do well if it arrived at midnight.

It was the coldest night we had had so far, with the moon practically full and shining from a cloudless sky and the frost sparkling brilliantly on the grass. We realised, of course, that we were feeling the cold all the more keenly, not only because we never got a hot meal, but also because our clothing by day was exactly the same as by night. The temperature at night warranted the addition of at least two pullovers, a scarf, an overcoat and a pair of gloves.

It must have been about 1 a.m. in the morning before that wretched train came. Whilst we did not imagine it was possible to be any colder, when we got inside and found, as usual, all the windows smashed in, we really began to realise what intense cold meant. How we stuck that night, I do not know, especially poor old Diffy, who for all his suffering, made less complaint than any of us. We seemed to go in all directions as we could tell by the constant shifting of the moon from one side of the train to the other. There was one point when we had to stand shivering for about an hour on a wayside station, waiting for a change of trains.

There was a short period of darkness after the moon had set, until the first grey streaks of dawn poured over the mountains to the east. Had we been in a better position to appreciate it, there is no doubt that the scene was one of wondrous beauty. However, I am afraid that by this time we all had one thought only – to get some warmth into our long-suffering bodies. It was quite light when we reached the station at Kirchundem, and a signpost immediately outside indicated that it was now 39 kilometres to Siegen. It was now nearly two days since the distance had been 100 kilometres, giving us a total distance covered of a mere 61 kilometres or 38 miles.

We had no doubt that our guards were equally as tired and in need of refreshment as we were, but nevertheless, the plan seemed to be to press on along what appeared to be the road to Siegen. It was obvious from the outset that the traffic along this road was going to be negligible. To me it seemed (and I warned the others of my conjecture) that from the lie of the land, we were in for a very long day's march. We were proceeding right up the side of a valley. As far as the eye could see in front, there appeared to be no real gap in the hills that held promise of any way out that would not involve a climb to a height of at least 2000 feet.

On and on up the valley we marched, until at length at about 9 a.m. we stopped in a small village and Karl said that he would enquire if there was any chance of our getting some coffee to drink with our breakfast. We ourselves thought it was about time that a move was made to give us some small additions to our diet. We were quite pleased, therefore, when eventually Karl led us into the front parlour of a house and we sat down and as well as the coffee, the housewife brought us some sandwiches made with tinned meat. This made a welcome change from the cheese diet and we were able to sweeten the coffee with a little saccharine from a small packet that one of the Russians had given me back in the prison at Werl.

1. Squire 'Tim' Scott.

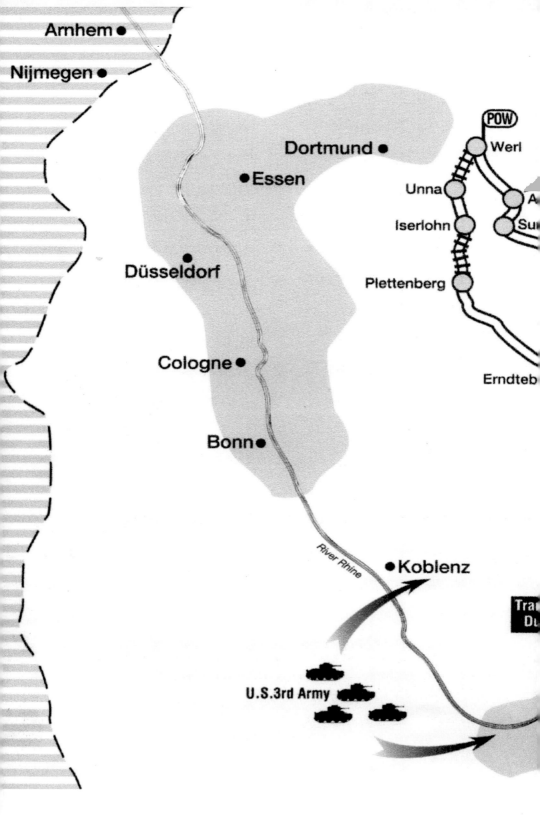

2. A map showing the route taken from capture to liberation by the American Third Army.

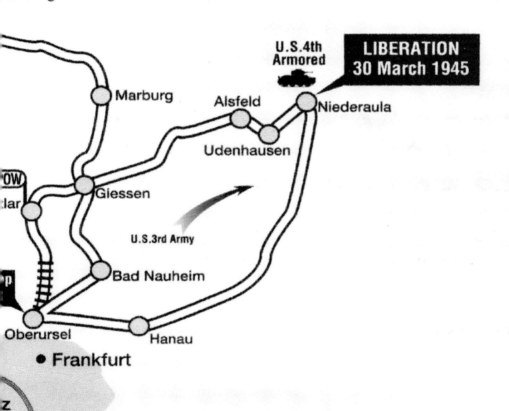

15 March 1945
id on Arnsberg
9 Squadron
nber Command

Landing & Capture

Kassel ●

lenberg

U.S.4th Armored

LIBERATION 30 March 1945

Marburg

Alsfeld

Niederaula

Udenhausen

OW

lar

Giessen

U.S.3rd Army

p

Bad Nauheim

Oberursel

Hanau

● Frankfurt

z

0mi   20   40   60

3. A photo taken of Scott's fellow crew members some time before the events described in this book. Those relevant to this story are: Alec James, pilot and skipper, centre back row; Jack Acheson, tail gunner, right back row; Ray Birch, radio operator, left front row

There was considerable activity during breakfast, with some Lightnings flying round and round the valley, no doubt after a particular target. We learnt a little later on that they had given a very good account of themselves, putting paid to the *bahnhof* that we had just left. Once again, fate had been with us.

Considerably refreshed, we carried on, always up hill and it was just about this time that Karl's left foot began to give him trouble. On more than one occasion we had to wait for him to catch up, for there was no doubt that Adolf still seemed to be in a desperate hurry and the pace, considering the warmth of the morning, was faster than any up to now.

We had one short stop where we hoped we might be allowed time for a little sleep, as we had had none the night before. However, we had no such luck and were forced on again as far as the picturesque village of Heinsberg, where Karl got some bandages for his foot from one of the villagers. Adolf led us out of this place without even waiting for Karl's treatment to be finished, leaving the old man to struggle behind as best as he could. It was a few minutes after that that Adolf had a bright idea, which (although he never knew it) was very nearly to cost him his life.

The road lay as I had forecast, right up the side of the mountain. From where we were, just outside Heinsberg, we could see the main highway proceeding in a series of four or five zigzags, until it disappeared into some woods nearly at the top. Adolf, with his usual ingenuity, found a footpath that went straight up the mountain side, avoiding all turns, and he indicated that we should follow this.

As was more or less to be expected, when he came in sight round a bend in the road, Karl kept straight on, instead of turning on to the footpath. Although we shouted to him, we could not make him hear and he was soon out of sight, taking in a loop that would obviously leave him a long way behind, unless we waited. Adolf, blissfully unaware that he was flirting with his own life, was determined that he was not going to wait.

CHAPTER EIGHT

Adolf's Narrow Escape

A dolf's short cut, to use an expressive but somewhat inapt simile, was 'like the side of a house'. The path found its way to the distant summit in a direct, uncompromising fashion.

The climb was sufficient to test the endurance of the fittest among us. In fact, before we got halfway up, it was obvious to me that I should not reach the top without a rest, whatever the condition of the others. Almost immediately, Arthur confirmed my opinion with a muttered oath, 'I'm b—d!' 'Me too,' I grinned, 'I'll lie down if you will.' In a few minutes, however, Adolf settled our problem by calling for a halt for '*essen*' by the side of a little stream. How thankfully we all flopped, and with a fair measure of relish, pulled out our all too familiar rations. By a unanimous vote, we decided that this was a special occasion and called for a departure from custom, in the form of an issue of both cheese and margarine for the meal. We felt that without taking into account what was yet to come, we had today used up more energy than on all the previous days put together!

We finished our sumptuous repast and washed it down with water from a stream. Adolf seemed to have acquired a water bottle at one of our halts during the morning – at any rate I had never noticed its presence before – and he now filled it for further use. We were all to be glad of a drink from that bottle in the next two or three days. Although, I can hardly think of anything, except possibly not being able to clean my teeth, which I detested more among our minor discomforts, than having to drink out of a bottle after dirty, filthy Adolf had used it.

Lunch over, we fell to discussing our plan. It was amazing how freely we talked about any subject under the sun, in front of Adolf. We even called him names to his face! We had fairly ample proof that his knowledge of English was even less than was ours of German. There he lay, ugly and sprawling on the grass, his tunic off, and his belt and revolver five yards away, discarded apparently with no thought of his responsibilities.

'Seems to me,' I said, 'that his nibs here would be damn glad if we made a bolt for it whilst his back was turned – he'd get to Frankfurt a whole lot quicker on his own.'

'Well, we could bump him off and dump him in the woods without a soul being any the wiser,' said Jack.

'We're not Germans,' I pointed out, 'and I am afraid it would take an awful lot of doing in cold blood.' Arthur and Diffy nodded their agreement with this.

'What we might do is to overpower him and cart him off into the woods until dusk, and then tie him up and hope he would not be able to make himself heard until daybreak. It's long odds we should get clean away because old Karl, whether he be fore or aft [I pointed expressively up and down the mountain], is going to be in no end of a stew when he fails to pick up with us again. He won't like putting in a report in any great hurry for fear of making a fool of himself.'

'What do you think of the idea of taking him along with us towards the Rhine?' said Jack.

'You mean threaten to shoot him if he tried to give us away,' I replied. 'The trouble would be that we would never be sure we could trust the blighter. If he once opened his mouth to a fellow Jerry, we'd never know, until it was too late, what he'd said!'

'No,' put in Arthur, 'and we'd never be able to get over to him what was required. I doubt if even our sign language would cope.'

During this interesting debate on his immediate future, our unsuspecting victim got up and strolled over to have a chat with the occupants of a cottage, a little way down the hill. As soon as he had left us, a Russian detached himself from a group we had observed, sitting round a fire about a hundred yards away. He sat down by our sides. We knew these fellows were Russians, because we had made former acquaintance with each other when we had met over the mutual task of gathering water from the stream. We wondered, however, what they were doing up here, all alone, and to all intents and purposes, their own masters.

This man did not speak any English, but he soon conveyed beyond any measure of doubt, the nature of his errand, which was to suggest that we slit the throat of Adolf without any further delay! If we did not fancy the job, he and his friends would do it for us free of all charge!

Poor Adolf! Wherever he may be now – and I doubt very much whether he ever saw a great deal of his wife in Frankfurt – he little knows how near his end was. The Russian went away and as Adolf wandered back, and began to collect his belongings, we made our decision to have a go. Only Diffy demurred, on the grounds that it was hardly worthwhile, as the war might only last another few weeks, and if we were caught again we should probably be shot.

I commented:

Well boys, I reckon with a wife and three kids, I have the most to lose if we don't make it, but it looks to me like an opportunity sent from Heaven. I suggest that as soon as we get clear of that cottage and the Russians, we trundle old Adolf off into the woods, lay up until tonight and then see how far away we can get before dawn comes, and with it, the possibility, but by no means certainty, that we shall be missed.

Diffy raised no more objections, and by now we were on our way round a slight corner in the path and out of sight of the cottage. The first sign of a hitch in the plan was the fact, obvious to us all, that the wood was becoming rapidly sparser. There was no stretch that would suit our purpose anything like as well as the one we had just left.

'Better be quick,' I said, not too brightly. Not only was the wood thinner, but it had receded further from the path, thus our deed had longer in which to be observed. 'Stop,' urged Diffy, 'there's a man up there.'

There was, too, about three hundred yards up the hill, and we blessed Diffy's sharp eyes. When we got up to the fellow and found he was only a Russian, we were not so sure! By that time, we could see the road coming into view away up on the right, and there was no telling what traffic might be on it, or who might have a grandstand seat for any performance enacted in the woods below. The circumstances had so changed since we conceived our great idea, that we one and all agreed with great reluctance to call it off. We may be thought to have been chicken-hearted, but we could see little future in being chased over Germany by a horde of hostile peasants. Lonely though the country was, I don't doubt that a surprising muster would soon have been in evidence had our deed been observed by but one person.

Considerably chastened, we at last reached the top of the hill and once more crossed the road. We looked up and down the road in vain for some sign of the errant Karl, who we remembered would have had no dinner, as Adolf was carrying both their rations. There was not the slightest hint as to whether he might be in front or behind us, but Adolf seemed quite unconcerned. He led us off down the other side at a cracking pace.

After about a couple of miles, we found that this side of the mountain was not as precipitous as the other. It soon opened out into a narrow valley, along which both our footpath and the main road followed parallel courses on opposite sides of a stream. The scenery, which all day had been of a high order, was now truly magnificent. I have always been a lover of nature, and it did me a lot of good to realise that here amongst my enemies, there were still things that were God's and were good. I counted myself lucky that in spite of all the circumstances, I still had the power in me to enjoy them. My pleasure was not, I fear, shared by those with whom I travelled. I was not about to ask Adolf, but the others showed little interest if I enthused over a particular scene or view, so after a while I gave up.

At long last, at about 3.30 p.m., we sighted Karl way ahead on the main road. Adolf let out an enormous shout, which made the old man turn round. Then we hastened down and across the stream, and on to the road to catch him up. He looked a comic and yet pitiable sight, reduced as he was, to walking in his slippers, because his feet were so bad. One hand clutched a stick, and over his other arm were slung his boots and his overcoat. He was hobbling along like a sick beast of burden and looking like anything other than a member of his beloved *Führer*'s police force.

We sat down for a rest by the roadside and there ensued the expected altercation between the two guards, who were naturally each trying to place the blame on the other, for the fact that they had been apart so long. Our interest at this stage was only academic, but we felt that had we been able, we ought to have put a word in on Karl's side, as the fault lay so plainly with the impatient Adolf.

Eventually, we pushed on again ever downwards towards, apparently, the town of Erndtebrück. The name of Siegen had not appeared on any further signposts since the one early this morning at Kirchundem, and we had found that this was not uncommon with German signposts. Maybe instead of taking them down altogether as the unenterprising English had done, the wily Hun thought it far better to keep them up, and make sure that the place on the signpost was never at the end of the road leading to it!

A mile or two further on, we stopped for Karl to have his lunch, and coffee was brought from a farm house for the whole party. It was during this break that our friends the Lightnings came again. We had hurriedly to take cover whilst they strafed a target that was very near at hand, but the location of which puzzled us afterwards for quite a time. It seemed to be just down the road and round the corner from where we sat, at most no more than half a mile away. However, although we had plodded on for fully two miles, we spotted no damage, until we learnt from Karl, who picked up the information from some civilians, that a train had been left with one truck sticking out of the end of a tunnel. The Lightnings had strafed the truck and rails and then placed a well aimed bomb right on the tunnel. Such was the job those gallant boys were doing during practically every minute of every day, whilst the first immense push over the Rhine was on.

It was just about this time, too, that we noticed the strange attitude of civilians towards the information volunteered by our guards that we were bound for Frankfurt. A typical conversation (translated by us with no knowledge of the language) would seem to go like this:

Civilian: 'Where have you come from?'
Adolf (who nearly always did the talking): 'Werl.'
Civilian: 'And where are you going to?'
Adolf: 'Frankfurt.'
Civilian: 'Frankfurt am Main?'
Adolf: 'Frankfurt am Main.'

The last would be the signal for all the civilians nearby to burst into hearty guffaws of laughter, in which it was noticed that Adolf did not join, although Karl smiled faintly. We, for our part, would have loved to have joined in the joke, but nobody seemed to want to let us in on it! We tried asking Karl, but for once the old man pretended he did not understand. How could we have guessed, that General Patton's Third Army had made such rapid progress in the period of just over a week since we had left home, that his spearheads were even now thrusting their way to the south to cut off this once fine city on the river Main.

Karl had his lunch, we all had coffee but did not have our third meal, and the Lightnings had their fun. Then in the cool of the evening, with today's trudge twelve hours old, we approached at last the town of Erndtebrück, covering the last 2 miles on the railway track. The track had come over the same mountain as we had, but by a slightly shorter route and making use of a now 'kaput' tunnel to get it clear of the last 500 feet or so. The pace had been so slow over the last 4 miles, due to the state of Karl's feet, that it was about 8 p.m. when we eventually picked our way over sets of obviously newly relaid metals and pulled up outside a patently *'kaput'* *bahnhof*.

We never thought for one moment that the pair had any idea of making us go any further without rest or sleep of some sort. We harangued old Karl about it in no uncertain terms, whilst Adolf made himself as busy as ever, enquiring about trains. The old man himself had obviously little relish for pushing on without rest, but he appeared to have little further authority. Very soon, Adolf was back announcing that there would be a train at 10 p.m.

The night was already growing bitterly cold; we were tired, hungry and, above all, very sleepy. By and large, we were in a state of advanced 'fed-upness'. In all our minds was the question 'What next?'

CHAPTER NINE

Getting a Move On

The answer was to be 'The mixture as before, only worse!' The only one thing that was certain was that there was not going to be any real rest. For a long time we wandered disconsolately in and out of the very much battered *bahnhof*, trying to discover if there was any part of it that was fit for human habitation. At last, a faint glimmer of light coming from the booking office told us that inside, there might at least be somewhere to sit, and it might not be as bitterly cold as it was outside. It was, I suppose, cheeky of us as prisoners to attempt to dictate where we should go. However, we knew that old Karl was quite soft-hearted, and would not see us suffer any more than was necessary, so we begged of him to enquire if we could park our weary bones inside the ticket office.

He agreed, and was successful. We filed in, however, the man and girl working in the office took very little notice. There was no fire, even in here, but it was a little warmer, and illumination was furnished by means of a single oil-burning lamp standing on a table in the middle of the room. We spotted a railway map hanging on a wall, and as nobody seemed to raise the slightest objection (I still think they would have been glad to see the back of us had we walked out there and then), we fell to studying it, both for possible further use, and with the immediate object of finding out exactly where we were. As I had anticipated, we were still not above halfway on our journey to Frankfurt, and we seemed to be about as near as we had ever been to that vital spot on the Rhine at Remagen, which was the only place within our knowledge where our Forces had made a crossing. What a thousand pities it was that we were not issued with a copy of the *Daily Mail* every morning!

We got our rations out. We were, I suppose, lucky to have anything to eat at all. However, the sight of that now very stale bread, the piece of cheese practically on its last legs, and the dirty slimy-looking mess that used to be margarine, could scarcely be considered as an appetiser for four men who had done a really hard day's footslogging. It was that or starve, though, and we knew that thousands had survived on far worse fare. We therefore made the best we could of it, washing the food down with a swig from Adolf's bottle, which he kindly handed round, as this poor derelict station seemed to be without water, in addition to its other shortcomings.

Our meal over, we tried to snatch a little sleep, but the room was steadily getting colder. Whilst Jack was soon snoring merrily with a heap of old sacks for a pillow, most of us found it very difficult to get sufficiently comfortable to doze off for more than a few minutes at a time. Diffy and I stood round the little lamp for quite a while, gathering what little bit of warmth we could from it, and talking about our situation. His wounds were showing some signs of healing, but he had a quite natural fear that the lack of nourishment in the food might cause them to turn septic, if they did not receive some proper treatment soon. The poor chap had been remarkably stoic, and seldom if ever complained, although he must have been in pain the whole of the time. He still adhered to his opinion that we should have been very unwise to have carried out our plot against Adolf during the afternoon, and I am not sure that, taking everything into account, he was probably correct.

The night dragged on, and it was probably about 1 a.m. before that wretched train came. By this time, as on the previous night, we were so cold as to be almost past caring, although we knew that in a few moments, when the usual corridor-type, windowless train got under steam, we should be a jolly sight colder. I don't think I'll ever forget that particular train journey – it just seemed like frozen eternity, combined with the agony with wanting to go to sleep. The desire was so desperate, that every few moments my head

would fall forward, and I would collapse off the
seat and into the lap of somebody sitting opposite
me. We were packed so tightly that it was
impossible for any save those sitting in the corners
to rest their heads anywhere, and I'm not sure
whether or not it was my own ineptitude, but I
never mastered the art of going to sleep unless my
head had definite support. It was sheer torture. I
don't know what my opposite number thought;
nothing was ever said, and every time I lunged
forward I just got pushed back again. I don't
know, either, what happened to the rest of our
crowd, for I never set eyes on one of them from
the moment we got in until, some three hours
later, we climbed out again out at a tiny wayside
station.

I was too dazed and stupified even to notice
where that station was, but I imagine it would be
one of those on the branch line north of Marburg,
for we were not long in passing through that town
in our subsequent travels. We set off on foot once
more, cold, stiff and indescribably weary. There
were many others going the same way, quite a few
going the opposite way, and a fair amount of
motor traffic. It was astonishing to see quite a
minor country lane so busy at 4 a.m. on what was
now Saturday morning, but I think by this time
we were beyond being surprised at anything that
these poor unhappy members of the Herrenvolk
chose to do in what was presumably in aid of their
beloved Fatherland's defence.

We walked on very slowly, far too slowly for all but Karl, whose feet were the factor that governed our pace. A horse-drawn cart passed us at a speed so little faster than ours that we were able to take a quick glance at its load, and craftily purloin a carrot apiece as a valuable addition to our rations! I was amazed at the feeling of elation that we experienced at thus having done a little something off our own bats to further our own ends. We noticed that two important crossroads that we passed were well guarded, and I remember wondering whether or not it would be easy to avoid such death traps if we were making our own way along in the dark in an attempted escape. In any case, it seemed but another pointer to the fact that the war was expected to come along this way pretty soon.

After about an hour we came to a small town. As was his wont, Adolf's first enquiry was for the *bahnhof*. '*Bahnhof kaput*', was the all too familiar answer, but nevertheless Adolf insisted on finding the station, so as to make sure for himself that this information was correct. He was soon out again, cursing fairly freely, and it was obvious that we should ride on no more trains tonight, for which we were more or less thankful, although we were as anxious as anybody to get this long journey over. We walked back along the road the way we had come, binding away at poor old Karl, who only smiled sadly and shook his head. Adolf, beyond a doubt, was supreme Commander-in-Chief, now!

We got back to the last crossroads about a mile out of the town, and Adolf set about putting in motion the machinery for a lift. It was 5 a.m., yet there was some traffic about, and in a very short time we were bundled aboard an open truck, which to our immense surprise Karl told us was going nearly all the way to Frankfurt. We were overjoyed – the cold seemed to be forgotten in the realisation that at last we looked like being able to get a move on. This truck seemed to be a modern speedy affair, and for a good three hours we ought to be free from the danger of interference by enemy aircraft. We all had seats of a sort, some on the floor, others on the sacks of wood that were used as fuel for nearly all the vehicles of this type.

We had an opportunity of studying the method of propulsion of our wagon a little more closely, when after a hard bitter non-stop drive, which lasted over two hours and must have knocked off a good 40 miles from our journey, we at last pulled up, and we were ordered to unload the sacks of wood. We hopped down into the road, glad of the chance to stretch our limbs. We watched the driver feed lumps of neatly chopped wood into a big cylinder, which stood up like a broad chimney at the rear of the driving cab on the right-hand side of the wagon. According to Jack, who used to be a bit of a chemist in his boyhood, the wood was burnt to charcoal, giving off an inflammable vapour known as producer-gas. It was this that was used as a substitute for petrol, to drive the motor. It all seemed very simple and very interesting, especially when we found that it was quite nice and warm standing in the road by the side of the bottom of the cylinder. We were not all displeased on discovering that it seemed to be necessary to wait for several minutes after filling up with wood. We made very good use of the time, in getting back into our ill-treated bodies a little of the heat that had been so freely expended during the night.

It was broad daylight by now, and the sun came up in a red fiery ball, giving the promise of yet another fine day, as we climbed back into our places, and the ride was resumed. We had passed through Marburg whilst it was barely light, and now almost immediately we came to Giessen (not to be confused with Siegen, which we never did get to), which is, or was, a railway town. Giessen had suffered at the hands of Allied bombers to an extent that had to be seen to be believed. It is a commonplace, and sometimes much over-exaggerated, description to say that there was not a building still standing. However, in the case of Giessen, I really believe it to be absolutely true, for the whole town was just one desolate mass of ruins. How any group of people could live through the many nights of death and destruction that this wholesale devastation must have required is a mystery to me. In fact, we all spent quite a bit of our time wondering why the German people as a whole did not take matters into their own hands and call a halt to this degradation of their country.

So that was Giessen, and our conveyance pressed on, sweeping at a good speed along a fairly clear road. We entered open country with the absence of the valleys and mountains of which we had seen so much that we had begun to think that all Germany was constructed to a single pattern. There was nothing further of note to catch our eye until we crossed one of the famous *Autobahn* a few miles north of Bad Nauheim. We had heard a great deal about Hitler's marvellous motorways, and had often noticed them from the air. But this was the first time we had seen one at close quarters, and we naturally found it quite interesting, though very little different from some of the big trunk highways at home, except for the novelty of the 'flyover' crossings.

A little while later, we came into Bad Nauheim itself. A woman in the truck who said she had a sister in America, and therefore spoke a little English, told us that it was a famous watering place. We came across the rather peculiar prefix 'Bad' quite often afterwards and assumed it to be the equivalent of our English 'spa'. This town had an air of quiet peace about it, and with its many buildings with a Red Cross on them, it appeared to have suffered very little from bomb damage. In a few more minutes, it would then be about 9.30

a.m., we arrived at Friedberg (pronounced exactly the same as our earlier Fredeberg), and were glad to be told that it was time for us to disembark.

Once more, Adolf was making a beeline at his best pace for the *bahnhof*. Whilst we glanced round rather anxiously at Karl, who was making no attempt to catch up, Adolf showed no concern at all. In fact, he was severely impatient with us for making any show at slowing the pace down so that Karl would be able to cope. When we thought that twelve hours ago we were still only halfway to Frankfurt, and now we showed signs of finishing the job off this morning, we could not but admire Adolf and his hustle. But we thought that it was very hard on poor Karl to be treated with such scant sympathy. We were a trifle annoyed ourselves that a bit more vim could not have been put into the earlier part of the trip, so that our efforts could have been more spread out and not all concentrated into this one last mad rush.

Still, ours was not to reason why. Adolf reached the *bahnhof* – there were no trains today. In a brief space of time, we had picked Karl up again and had started off down the road towards a place call Bad Homburg. Karl told us that the *Stalag* to which we were being taken was actually at Oberursel, some 10 miles on this side of Frankfurt. A few minutes later, we quite unexpectedly said 'Goodbye' to him, as it appeared to have been arranged between the guards that with Karl's feet in the condition they were, he could not possibly tackle what would devolve into another full day's march if we did not get a lift. There was still, it seemed, another 20 miles to go.

Our party reduced to five, we were incredibly fortunate in getting a lift almost as soon as Karl left us, for the road seemed have little traffic. It was a covered truck, and the only other passengers appeared to be two land girls. They spent the whole journey with their heads stuck through the canvas, keeping their eyes open for enemy activity in the skies. Fortunately, there was no adverse incident. By about 10.30 a.m., we had passed through Bad Homburg, and our conveyance had set us down in the very pleasant little town of Oberursel. There was no sign at all of any damage by bombs, and we recalled clearly how, when we ourselves had been briefed to attack Frankfurt one night, we had been given very strict instructions to be careful of the POW camp, which lay about 10 miles to the north of the city. Well, by the look of it, all the crews had carried out their order very conscientiously.

We started to remind Adolf again about *essen*. We had tried to attract his attention back at Friedberg, but he would have none of it then. Now he indicated that we must push on a little bit towards the *Stalag*, which by this time seemed as though it ought to be pretty near at hand, thanks to the enormous hustle of the last few hours. We accordingly asked for the loan of his knife, and proceeded to peel and eat our carrots, which tasted very good as a change from bread and cheese. In a few more minutes, Adolf indicated a grassy patch by the side of a tram track, and we were able to have our first meal for well over twelve hours. A civilian woman brought us a few small and very over-ripe apples, which tasted quite good. What with these, and the carrots, and the fact that we felt justified in clearing up the whole of the cheese in what just about amounted to a double ration all round, we felt that we were indulging in a feast almost fit for a king – almost!

Breakfast over, we boarded one of the quaint little trams that seemed to emanate from Frankfurt. After a short ride through the outskirts of Oberursel, we at last came to the gates of the prison camp. We surveyed the place with interest as we walked the last 50 yards towards the sentry box. It was very pleasantly situated, as had been the one at Arnsberg. There were neat rows of wooden huts all lined up on the side of a hill slope, with pine woods in the rear to lend a picturesque touch to the background. We noticed the fact, which was as obvious as it had been at Arnsberg, that there was no sign of any English or American prisoners! Our first flush of excitement was over and doubtfully, with quickly growing misgivings, we entered.

CHAPTER TEN

Journey's End

Adolf was soon fussing about from one official to the other, but even whilst he was thus occupied, the conviction in our minds grew to a certainty that this place was not to be for us. After a little while, we were led into a room that was once somebody's office but which now appeared as though its occupants were in the throes of packing-up ready to move on. We were invited to sit on a little bed that stood against one wall, and a *Luftwaffe* corporal addressed us in English.

'This camp is no more,' he said, 'you will have to go on to Wetzlar, and there is one other to go with you.' As he spoke, our eyes turned to the door, and we beheld an English flight sergeant air gunner, with no shoes on his feet. He looked every bit as weary as us. The corporal left the room, and Jack Evans, for that was his name, joined us on the bed. He told us that he had baled out a week ago yesterday, which was the day after our accident, and that he had managed to evade for five days before at last getting picked up due to making an over-confident appearance in the daylight. He had lost one of his boots in the jump, and whilst he still carried the other one over his shoulder, he had spent most of the time barefoot – a state of affairs that had not done a lot to alleviate the natural sufferings of his predicament.

Like ourselves, he had hoped that his arrival at Oberursel meant at last a relief from immediate hardship. He was immensely disappointed that he still had to face a further period of unknown duration, on the road, especially as the powers-that-be were either unable, or unwilling, to furnish him with a pair of boots. At length, the arrival of lunch, in a more appetising form than of late, of a tin of meat that looked like spam, with some fresh bread and margarine, cheered us all up.

There was an incident over lunch that showed up Adolf's petty character. Ever since we had lost Karl, we had had difficulty in cutting the bread, because Adolf's penknife was not really adequate. Accordingly, I borrowed a table knife from the English-speaking corporal for our own use, on the understanding that if he were not there when we finished, it was to be left on the table. On the completion of the meal, Adolf calmly wiped the knife and put it among his own possessions, taking no notice of our remonstrations that it was only borrowed. Although the victim was a German, we felt that our honour was at stake. Rather than let Adolf get away with it, we wrote a little note, leaving it on the table where the corporal would see it on his return. It read:

Dear Corporal,
   The knife we borrowed has been removed by our guard, and not by us.

It might appear utterly trivial and ridiculous that it should bother us, but it shows the innate honesty of the average British mind.

We didn't see that corporal again, for in a little while an officer appeared, and indicated that with Adolf once more as our guard, we were to proceed immediately to Wetzlar. Adolf was obviously disappointed that his visit to his wife was to be delayed still further. Yet, he retained all his cunning, for we sensed that he was telling the officer that another guard would not be necessary as he could pick up Karl again in Frankfurt, where it seemed, he had, in any case, arranged to meet him at the railway station. Crafty fellow, all he was worried about was retaining charge of the party so that he could make his own pace.

We set off down the road once more. Jack Evans, whom we arranged to call 'Ev' so as to avoid confusion with the other Jack, plodded along in his bare feet. We boarded one of the quaint little trams, and soon were once more in the town of Oberursel, with Adolf making his usual beeline for the *bahnhof*. It was a nice modern unbombed station and according to the timetables still hanging around everywhere, it must have handled an enormous number of trains to all parts of Germany in the days before our Air Force got busy. There was actually a current timetable, the first we had seen on any of the many stations we had visited. It indicated, according to Adolf, quite accurately, that there were no trains at all to Frankfurt, and none to anywhere else before 7.15 p.m.

Whether or not it was consideration for Ev's feet we could not be sure but Adolf seemed disinclined for further activity on the road. He said that we would wait for the train, which would take us towards Wetzlar, and we should have to give poor old Karl the go-by. We didn't fancy waiting on the *bahnhof* and asked if we could find somewhere for a sleep. We were mindful, and I expect Adolf was too, for he agreed readily enough, that we had not had anything approaching a night's sleep since the night before we had left Werl, which was Monday. It was now Saturday. After a short walk round the houses, we at last found a grassy patch by the side of the tramtrack, and settled ourselves for a quiet, lazy afternoon until it was time for our train.

On and off, we managed a little sleep. It was rather hard on Adolf being the sole guard, because when it had got to about 4.30 p.m. and we had all slept and were sitting up again talking, he lay down. Unable to keep awake any longer, he was soon snoring loudly. I suppose it was rather a dirty trick, but we couldn't resist it, and when a German warrant officer came along, we pointed to Adolf, then to ourselves, five desperate POWs. We indicated how absurd we thought it was that we should be sitting there whilst he indulged himself in the luxury of sleep! The outcome was that poor old Adolf was rudely awakened from his dreams and given a thorough telling off, with the five of us looking on, not understanding a word of what was said, but realising that Adolf was getting it hot and strong!

After he had exhausted his invective, and with Adolf looking more crestfallen than we had ever seen him before, the warrant officer turned to us. Finding that we understood a little French, he stayed and talked to us for quite a while. We explained that our American friend had been severely knocked about by the civilians, and we thought we were entitled to a little better protection than was to be obtained from one guard who went to sleep whenever the fancy took him. He agreed and said that we ought to have another. We found, too, that this fellow was one of the very few Germans whom we had come across who really seemed to think that the war would last a lot longer (his estimate was two years) and that Germany had any chance of winning.

When, at last, he went on his way, we decided to have tea. As now our rations had been augumented by two more loaves of bread, some margarine and two tins of spam, we felt that we could indulge in a better meal, for we gathered from Adolf that the journey to Wetzlar ought not to take above another twenty-four hours. So we tucked in, and washed the meal down with water given to us over the fence by the kindly inhabitants of a nearby house. As we ate we could hear the sound of gunfire not very far away. Although it seemed incredible to us at the time, we were prepared to swear that the sound was coming from other directions besides the west, whence we would normally expect it. Had we but known it, even as we sat there eating our meal of bread and spam, General Patton's merry men must have been creeping up on Frankfurt from the south and east. However we had been too long out of touch with any reliable news even to know that the Rhine had been crossed as far south as this.

At about 6 p.m. we returned to finish off our long wait at the *bahnhof*. It was there that Jack relayed the information that he said he had got from some Russians he had met in the lavatory, that the American armies were within 15 kilometres of Oberursel. It seemed fantastic, and yet the news was probably quite true. At the same time, it was sufficient to set our minds roving once more in the directions of plans for escape. From experience of previous nights, it appeared that it would be a relatively easy matter to drop off the train during the night, because with only one guard to bother about now, there would almost surely be a time when he would fall asleep. Once we had gone, the big advantage would be that he would not know at which station we had disappeared. We talked about it a great deal during the long wait for the train, but we were aware that Adolf (presumably with the warrant officer's words still ringing in his ears) was keeping a much more careful eye on us than hitherto. He had actually counted us on two occasions, a formality than neither he nor Karl had ever bothered with before.

At about 8.30 p.m. the train pulled in, and as soon as we entered we got a very rude shock, for it actually seemed to be warm! There were real glass windows in all the compartments, and whilst the warmth was only natural, probably because the coach had been standing in the sun all afternoon, there was plenty of room, and we were able to spread ourselves in a manner that promised some sleep for a change. What was beneficial for sleeping was not so good for escaping, however, because with there being ample accommodation, Adolf was able to position himself so that he could keep a watchful eye on all of us the whole time.

We had surmised on previous occasions that some of these trains went an awful long way round to get to their destinations. Tonight we were treated to a concrete example of the utter chaos existent in the railway system. The journey from Oberursel to Bad Homburg, which, by the main line, was no further than 3 miles (and which was scheduled, on the old timetables, to take five minutes), took a full thirty-five minutes at quite a fair speed, and with no intermediate stops.

We rode for a very considerable distance in this train. Its initial warmth was beginning to wear off, when at last it pulled up in the open country, and all the passengers were ordered to alight. Following our guard, we marched at a brisk pace along a path running by the side of the single track. In a few minutes we came across what was to us a most beautiful sight, and the cause of the diversion became obvious. The track, quite suddenly, as though tired of running straight and level on its stoney bed, climbed at a gradient of about one in two until it reached a height of about 12 feet from the ground. There, it left off altogether and the broken ends looked down sorrowfully on a neat round hole, some 12 yards in diameter. On the opposite side, the missing section of metal ran down into the hole, and then up one of the sides, over the top, and then it disappeared into a ditch. Altogether, we were most impressed by what undoubtedly was an extremely accurate piece of bombing, the more so because no women or children would have been killed. Our friends the German civilians who caused us so much trouble in the town, would in this case be deprived of one of their most popular gibes.

When the line was at last safe, we found another train drawn up to receive us, and we were quite astounded at this evidence of a high degree of organisation to meet the dire needs of the circumstances. We climbed on board, and as expected, found we were back in the old windowless type again. As it was now only about 11 p.m., we wondered just how many hours of freezing we were going to be asked to endure. After this train had been steaming for about a couple of minutes it stopped again. There was then a long wait, the purpose of which was entirely obscure, until at last along the road could be seen two or three women pushing prams. Obviously, it would have been impossible to navigate the prams along the rough footpath and over the bombed stretch. Give Jerry his due, he thought of everything and everybody!

We had not talked any more about the chances of organising an escape. In this new train, we also found that the accommodation was limited, and we were spread out over half a coach, and so got no further chance to discuss the matter. Any one man could have gone when he liked and would never have been missed until the final disembarkation. Diffy told me afterwards that several times he felt tempted to try, but something held him back. I think it must have been that strange something that made me refrain from making a dash for it too. Perhaps something amounting to a Divine inspiration told me that the best thing to do was to hang on and wait for the right moment to turn up.

It had got to about 1 a.m., and we were nothing like as cold as on the previous nights (in fact, we thought that the night itself was a little warmer) when we were ordered off the train again. Adolf was once more trying his luck with the local *bahnhof*. The one we were at was out of use, it seemed, but there might be a habitable one at Weilburg, which was about 3 kilometres away. We set forth, and soon reached the town, but it was a long, straggly kind of place, and it took us an awfully long time, wandering up and down the streets, before we found the station. Adolf, meanwhile, had evidently some hopes of travelling a bit by road, for he stopped quite a few vehicles that passed our way, without finding anything going to Wetzlar. We saw a signpost that gave the distance as 27 kilometres, and wondered whether eventually we should have to walk it.

At length we located the *bahnhof*, bombed out and out of use as usual. There were no trains in evidence, and not the slightest chance of there being any, from what we could gather. It was growing very cold again, and there was one room on the station that was inhabited. It smelt warm and inviting, and seemed to be in use as a kind of club for travelling officers. We supposed, quite rightly, that we should not be invited to share the comfort of this apartment, but Adolf dived inside. In a few moments' he reappeared with a young officer who was apparently going to show us where warmth and shelter could be obtained. He led us round the corner and down a flight of stone steps into a hot, filthy and stinking dungeon, where a crowd of men, who for the most part looked like lorry drivers, were stretched out on stone benches trying to get some sleep.

It really was a fearful place. The heat was provided by a large stone fireplace in one corner, and among the men present were some of the toughest, dirtiest and most unhealthy-looking specimens that I saw during the whole of my stay in the Reich. One felt that if one went to sleep, it was a toss-up whether one would be allowed to wake up again. However, we reflected that they probably knew our status, and considered we should not be worth robbing anyway. Nevertheless, it was depressing to a degree, and whilst most of us managed to snatch a little sleep, we were not sorry when at about 4.30 a.m. Adolf gave us our marching orders once again.

The difference in temperature when we came out was appalling, and it was a wonder that we did not all catch pneumonia on the spot. We fretted up and down in what shelter was offered by the bombed out station booking hall, whilst Adolf did his stuff out in the road, with what few lorries were passing by. He had a long spell, but at length came back. He indicated that it was no use and we should have to walk. Jack Evans at once avowed that he was not going to walk 27 kilometres in his bare feet. He sat down on the floor, produced a pocket knife, and proceeded to make himself a pair of sandals out of the one whole flying boot that he still carried around with him. The resource and ingenuity of that fellow were amazing, but I still could not help commenting on the fact that had he been prompted to do this before, at the very beginning of his ordeal, he would have had plenty of time to spare then, and his need must have been even more pressing than it was now. I'm afraid that I did not get any satisfactory answer to my comment!

It would be about 6 a.m. when at last he was set up with a quite workable pair of sandals, and we were able to get some warmth into our systems by steady walking. Whilst we might start off at a good average speed of about 5 kilometres an hour, we knew from previous experience that our average would soon deteriorate. We felt that if we accomplished the full journey by teatime, we should do quite well. We started to bind pretty early about *essen*, for we had not eaten for over twelve hours. Adolf was adamant that we continue, however, and we gathered that we should have to wait two or three hours until it got warmer.

The Thunderbolts were out early that morning. We soon got quite a scare, because we had got mixed up with a 'convoy' of Russian and Italian prisoners who were being marched to some distant destination, and we were afraid that our friends up in the P47s would mistake us for a retiring column of German soldiers. Twice around 8 a.m. we were forced to retire ignominiously into the ditch. On the second occasion, the aircraft dived down so close to us that we felt certain they must have been aiming for us. They had a target just out of sight round the bend in the road, however, and we were able to breathe freely once again, when at last their mission was accomplished and they flew away.

At about 9 a.m., when it was at last beginning to get quite warm, we stopped in a little wood just off the side of the road, and began another meal of bread and spam. We had no water, except the drop that was left in Adolf's bottle which to give him his due, he was not at all selfish about, and made no demur at passing round. When I think about it now, it really was a marvel that we all did not contract all sorts of vile diseases, the way six of us drank quite unconcernedly out of the one dirty water bottle. Yet, at the same time, it was amazing that men, living under the most unsanitary and primeval conditions as we were, could flout all the known laws of hygiene and yet survive unscathed to tell the tale. It is I suppose, again, that same Divine hand.

We could see the trend of our road as it stretched for what promised to be many a hot and dusty mile along the side of a broad open valley, which was utterly devoid of any scenic merit when compared with the charming countryside encountered on our full day's hike on Friday. The walk that followed was also completely lacking in noteworthy incident, and long before the day was out we were weary of it. We made one quite long stop during the morning for Ev to bathe his feet in a stream, and Adolf improved the shining hour by having a shave. We had two subsequent halts to collect water from friendly cottagers, and when it came to a question of a stop for lunch, once again we could not get our guard to see that we English folk liked to keep our meals to regular hours! He was quite determined to get within sight of the place, before allowing us to eat again.

At about 2.30 p.m. there were signs that we might be getting near our journey's end, for with Wetzlar still 4 kilometres away according to the milestones (or rather kilometrestones), we came across a number of *Luftwaffe* personnel who looked suspiciously like prison guards. At any rate, a check of some sort was in progress and Adolf had to produce his papers. I confessed to a certain feeling of astonishment, not only that he had them, but also that they appeared to be in order! These men pointed out a short cut, for we at once left the road and climbed up into the grounds of an old country house, which was a prominent landmark some 200 feet above the surrounding countryside. We wondered if this was the place we were aiming at. Our hearts began to sink again, for there were no signs of any prisoners, but we passed right through the grounds and out on the other side into a ploughed field.

'*Zwei kilometres – essen*' said Adolf, holding up two fingers. We flopped tharkfully into the dirt, gathering that we could eat now, our last meal with the worthy Adolf, and it would only take us about a further twenty minutes to complete the journey. We had the additional company as we ate of two small boys, who kept rubbing their hands together and grinning, as though anticipating for us a gruesome fate in the *Stalag* that lay just over the hill. It all looked reasonably authentic this time, and we wondered what might be in store for us.

The meal over, we pushed on. At last, on breasting a ridge, we could see the camp with its large white POW letters standing out on the roofs of two of the buildings, over on the next ridge, about half a mile away. The approach was a bit roundabout, but we eventually drew into sight of the main entrance. We were greatly cheered at seeing many men in American and British uniforms sitting and strolling around the grounds.

Adolf handed us over without loss of time and beat a hasty retreat, presumably lest he was required for a further job and his visit home should be delayed still more. Goodbye, Adolf, you treated us pretty well, on the whole. I hope that you got to Frankfurt before the Americans, and that old Karl was still waiting for you on the railway station! Does it seem a very strange thing to record that our hearts were light as we passed within the prison gates, and that after we had been inside the place a couple of hours we had but one word with which to describe it, and that was 'Heaven'?

CHAPTER ELEVEN

Dulag Luft

The feeling of elation that clutched at our hearts came from the knowledge that at last we could stop being nomads for a little while, we could almost surely find some sort of a bed on which to secure a semblance of a proper night's rest, and surely the food would be no worse than what we had been getting. Indeed, if there were any Red Cross parcels coming through, it ought to be a jolly sight better. The description 'Heaven' came to be applied when we found that the amenities were far in excess of what we expected, even in our most optimistic moments. When we came to compare our possible future as POWs with what we had been through, there just did not appear to be any other word that fitted. Had we but known how short was to be our stay … !

We parted company with Adolf and were led into a room where there was every evidence of a brisk organisation fully laid on to deal with our very case. We were thoroughly searched and subjected to a brief interrogation by an English-speaking official. He was not at all inquisitive, and quite understood the rule of 'Number, rank and name only'. He had heard it, he said with a smile, many times before! Our photographs were taken, and we were then led away to the clothing store, where we met a Wing Commander Kelly who was in charge. It seemed very strange to be talking to an official who was not a German, but he thought nothing of it, and was soon dealing with our requirements in much the same way as if we had been a bunch of new recruits at a Receiving Centre back at home. We were all issued with a clean shirt, long woollen underclothing, socks, half a towel and other little amenities such as soap, razor blades, cigarettes and toothpaste. These things were an everyday matter in a civilised community, but we had almost forgotten their very existence. I also changed my shoes for another pair, which were a little too big for me and nearly as worn as the ones I discarded. I also received a big warm American flying jacket for use as an overcoat. Most of this stuff we learnt was supplied through the American Red Cross.

As pleased as kiddies with new toys we followed an American POW, who appeared to have been detailed to look after us, along to the showers. After a doctor had given us a brief inspection, chiefly for lice, we were able to enjoy the indescribable luxury of a hot shower. Every minute underneath the sizzling spray seemed to atone for the hours of discomfort and misery spent in acquiring the dirt and filth that was now so rapidly slipping away under the soothing influence of soap and hot water. Afterwards, although I personally loathed long-legged underpants and long-sleeved vests, it was a real pleasure to feel something next to the skin that was clean.

As soon as we were ready, our guide told us to go and get some tea, and we joined a queue at the building he indicated as being the mess hall. The Germans supplied a bare ration of bread and potatoes, and everything else we ate at that sumptuous repast was the product of the American Red Cross. That was the first time, but it was destined to be by no means the last, that I had occasion to offer unstinted praise to the Americans and the way they organised supplies of food. It really was by comparison, a feast. We had a kind of stew made with tinned turkey, with the German potatoes and bread to take away the richness. This was followed by half a packet each of lucious dates, of the kind which had been practically non-existent for many years back in England. We also had very appetising biscuits and cheese and hot sweet cocoa. We were warned by men sitting at our table not to eat too heartily, if we had been living on short rations for a long spell. But for all that we had a really enjoyable meal, and rose, if a trifle heavier, at least a whole heap lighter-hearted. Such is man and his tummy!

We learnt that the mess hall and kitchen were run by volunteers from among the prisoners. No work of any kind was expected from us other than to take up our cup and plate to the servery. We could, if we wished, volunteer to help in the kitchen, but according to our informers there was always a long waiting list! We felt that for a few days, at any rate, we should be quite content to do absolutely nothing! We were most disappointed to learn that the camp. Dulag Luft, to give it its correct title, was only a sorting out centre, and that nobody ever stayed more than a week. A transport had left only that morning for Nüremberg, it seemed, and the total number of able-bodied men still on the camp was probably fewer than 100. Further enquiry elicited the information that the term 'transport' was only a polite fiction, being the equivalent to the English 'posting'. The men had left on foot, in much the same manner as they had arrived.

Rumour seemed pretty rife among our fellow prisoners that the whole camp was shortly due to pack up and move to quarters more remote from the advancing Allied armies. This news did not surprise us at all. In view of our experience to date, we had been astonished that it had not moved before we arrived there! We were subjected to a bombardment of questions as to our adventures *en route*, and there was a particular anxiety to learn if we had any fresh news on the progress of the war. The prisoners got a daily bulletin from the Germans, but naturally only got told as much as was good for them, and relied to a large extent on incoming men to give them the up-to-date news. We were only able to tell them of the rumour we had heard that the Americans were supposed to be within 15 kilometres of Oberursel last night. This seemed to tally with similar information brought in by somebody else, and everybody got fairly excited.

We had orders to stay in the mess hall for the time being, as there was an air raid in progress over the town of Wetzlar, about 2 miles away. This gave us the chance to spend quite a long while chatting to different fellows and getting to know as much as we could about our new surroundings. At length we moved out, collected up our few belongings and made our way to the barrack store. Here, we were issued with no fewer than four blankets each – again a vote of thanks was due to the American Red Cross. We were shown to our billets and found that these, although crowded, were clean and tidy, and the prospect of a decent night's sleep loomed large and happily in front of us. There were eight three-tier bunks in the room, making accommodation for twenty-four men. I often smiled afterwards when I recalled our joy at finding that we should have a whole bunk to ourselves. Back at base we would have been disgusted if we had been offered a portion of even a two-tiered bed in which to pass a single night, in for example, the emergency of a diversion to a different airfield.

We five comrades were all together in the one room, although Diffy had been missing for some time. We gathered that he had been over to the hospital to get proper treatment for his wounds. Our room-mates, as ever, were a mixed crowd, but there seemed some very decent fellows among them, and once more we were soon busy swapping yarns. We learnt that nobody was allowed out of the building after 8 p.m., by which time it was practically dark. We thought that this arrangement would suit us very well, as by that time we hoped to be fast asleep in our nice cosy little bunks! I don't know what the others did, but I remember that by 7.30 p.m., I was in bed. In a very short space of time, the noise of the chatter had faded away, and I knew no more until somebody was murmuring that it was time to get up. I felt under my pillow for the watch that wasn't there, wondering vaguely whether it was an early call for 'ops' that morning. Then, with a violent start, I realised where I was. Somebody who had the fortune to possess a watch, announced that it was 7.15 a.m., and we all ought to be getting out of bed.

I suppose that each one of us spent the day in his own different way. I, for my part, made up my mind very early that just in case we were going to be moved on in a big hurry, I would get in as much rest as possible, because there was no doubt that, although like the others, I felt reasonably fit, the vicissitudes of the past eleven days had used up a good deal of my reserve energy.

As we were dressing, I got hold of a good deal of information from the English flight sergeant navigator, Harry, who occupied the bunk immediately above me.

'What time do we have breakfast?' I asked.

'It's a quarter past seven now,' he replied, 'and by eight o'clock, you have to be washed and shaved, blankets have to be folded and we all have to be outside for roll-call. Immediately afterwards, we eat.'

'And what happens after that?'

'After that, you come back here and if it is fine, you are supposed to shake your blankets out of doors, tidy up the room and the rest of the morning is your own.'

'That will suit me fine.' I said. 'What about dinner?'

'Dinner is at 12 noon and after that there is nothing else to do until roll-call just before tea, at 4.30.'

By this time we had finished dressing and my friend showed me where we could wash. It was all nice and clean and pleasant, although there was no hot water. Using the razor I had acquired, I managed to scrape off a further accumulation of four days' beard. When I had finished this feat of endurance, it was breakfast time. Hastily pushing my blankets into some form of order, I joined the others in the parade outside.

This was the first time that I had any opportunity of studying the occupants of the camp as a whole. I found that everybody who could walk was expected to attend this parade for roll-call, although there were some poor chaps limping around on crutches and others with their heads bandaged or their arms in slings.

There was no attempt made at calling all the names, but a rapid count of those present was taken and presumably as long as the numbers tallied, this was sufficient. There was hardly any formality attached to the gathering and as soon as the count had been made, we received the order to dismiss, which was also the signal for everybody to scamper into the mess hall.

Breakfast again, no thanks to the Germans, was a meal equally as good as supper the night before. I was still in conversation with my new friend Harry and during breakfast I picked up a few more facts about life in the prison camp.

'Does anybody try to escape?' I asked him.

'Nobody ever wants to,' was the reply. 'It's far too comfortable here. There was a case though, the other day, of a fellow who got through the barbed wire somehow and ran across the fields in broad daylight and, of course, he was shot instantly by one of the guards up in the tower. He must have been mad; the guard simply couldn't miss at the range.'

'Are the guards very strict then?'

'No – most of them are fairly decent easy-going fellows, but they nearly all speak English, so you want to be careful what you say.'

'You needn't worry, I'm not going to say anything. I am just going to lie down and go to sleep – is there a library here?'

'Yes, there is a very good one' said Harry. 'I think it opens at 10 a.m. and they have got stacks and stacks of books. You can get a new one every day if you want.'

'It is all Red Cross stuff, I suppose?'

'Yes. We are among the lucky ones here. The Red Cross parcels have never stopped coming and I believe they have got enough grub to last for months, even if the Germans never issued any more at all. As a matter of fact, they say this Camp is the best in Germany.'

'And they say we may be going tomorrow,' I groaned, 'just our so-and-so luck'.

Breakfast over, we returned to the billet and as it was just starting to rain, somebody said that we would not need to shake out our blankets. This seemed to suit everyone and they all settled down to employ themselves in their different ways. Playing cards were available and two games were soon going on the table in the middle of the room. Arthur said that he was going to do some washing, which I agreed was not a bad idea, although it looked as though, with the first wet day we could remember in many weeks, it was going to be a job to get the stuff dry. I compromised by washing my pants and vest, because I didn't feel that I was going to be able to stick the service issue for very long. I hung these on the end of the bed, waiting for the rain to stop.

When Arthur and I came back to the room, it seemed that we had been rather lucky in being away for a few minutes. During our absence the chief Allied officer, who was a big red-faced American colonel with a terrific bark but very little bite, had been round and insisted that all blankets be taken outside and shaken, rain or no rain. Arthur and I felt terribly lazy and as we had missed hearing the instruction, we felt quite justified in ignoring it. We were sure that our blankets, only having been issued the night before, could not possibly need shaking yet!

My day's work was done and I strolled round to the library leisurely and whilst waiting for it to open studied a specimen postcard supplied by the Red Cross for sending to the folks at home to let them know what was going on. This specimen must have been read by many thousands of prisoners passing through the camp in the past. No doubt they had all got a good laugh out of the imaginary American soldier who was writing to his sweetheart back in New York and telling her not to worry about 'Junior', as they would be married as soon as he got home. I made a mental note that I must get my own postcard fixed and despatched as soon as possible.

I secured my book *Random Harvest*, and spent the remainder of the day in luxurious idleness, lying on my bunk and alternatively reading and dozing. Dinner time came quite rapidly and the meal was as good as its predecessor; during the afternoon there was a break of about an hour when we had to go down into the shelters, because Wetzlar was again being heavily raided by our bombers. It was damp and cold in the shelters, but we all felt that it was in a very good cause and nobody was at all disposed to grumble. About teatime the sun came out, and with it, Arthur's and my washing. We were able to spend the remaining few hours of daylight after tea sitting or strolling around the grounds in the same manner as those whom we had seen on our arrival the day before.

It was all very pleasant and our troubles and cares of the earlier days seemed very remote. One reads so much of POWs who have suffered to an unimaginable extent by years spent behind barbed wire with nothing to do. Whilst it is easy to realise how one could eventually get to this stage, it is at the same time difficult to make it sufficiently clear how completely overwhelmed we were by the sheer luxury of being absolutely idle.

Dusk came and in accordance with the regulations, we retired once more to our billets. I joined in a game of bridge with Diffy and Jack and a young American officer. I am afraid that none of us could work up a great deal of enthusiasm, as the novelty of being able to go to bed had not worn off and we were all really quite anxious to have another early night, while the chance was there. One of the big advantages that I found these barrack rooms had over our Nissen huts back at base, was the fact that lights had to be out at 10 p.m. and there was no disposition as was often the case at home, for some of the fellows to want to talk until well into the small hours. Everybody was in bed and asleep by the time the lights were turned off, and as on the previous night, we all slept like logs. Unfortunately, when we were awakened by a loud voice outside in the passage imploring us to get up at once, it didn't seem, from the colour of the sky outside, that it was anything like the normal rising time!

CHAPTER TWELVE

March out of Wetzlar

The gentlemen with the watch announced that it was 5 a.m. There was a lot of shouting and grumbling going on from the other fellows and we soon learnt that our orders were to pack and we were to leave immediately. When we visualised our few belongings, we considered that the word 'pack' was hardly appropriate. It seemed that there was a set method laid out of wrapping up one's belongings into the two ends of a rolled up blanket, in such a fashion that it could be worn across the shoulders with little or no inconvenience. There was a plan hung up on the wall at the entrance to the barrack block, showing exactly how this should be done. As the guards seemed to be in a desperate hurry for us to get moving, there was much frantic scambling up and down by the fellows who had their stuff out on the floor at the far end of the passage and who were anxious to have the thing done in the proper manner. The system seemed to need a fearful amount of room in the initial stages, as the blanket had to be laid out flat, and the chaos that existed with people charging up and down the passage, trampling over each other's blankets and kicking one another's possessions all over the place, can be imagined.

Amid the general confusion and hubbub, German guards were dashing in and out shouting at us in their best English to hurry up and get outside.

'We move at once,' said one guard in a strange, dull monotone that was to become one of the most familiar sounds to us in the days that followed.

I managed my pack in fair style, remembering at the last minute to snatch my washing off the line and to remind Arthur about his. I joined the growing crowd outside, just in time to hear my name called. It seemed, even then, that although everybody, whatever his state of health, had been got out of bed and forced to line up outside, only those whose names were called and who were fit, were going to travel. The out-going party were ordered to line up in a fresh group by the main gates. When at last we were in something like order, a count was taken and it was found that there were eighty-two of us. Our American Colonel gave us a short address and told us to take heart, as it was quite possible that we should be back in the camp that evening He did not appear to be going with us, although we had two Wing

Commanders as well as an American Major in our party.

We were issued with a supply of chocolate and cigarettes and then at the last moment, it seemed that there was a hitch about food, as the Germans were alleged only to have enough for their own men. Apparently on an impulse, the Colonel ordered us to be supplied with a full American Red Cross parcel each. We thought that at least we ought not to starve for a few days, but carrying the parcel was causing everyone concern, as it was quite heavy and rather bulky for placing under the arm. For those of us who had the material, a piece of string tied round the box provided a temporary, although not very efficient, solution.

Outside the gates, the contingent of German guards and members of the *Luftwaffe* were also getting themselves organised. There seemed to be a very large number of them and they had two or three trucks with their equipment on. One very large vehicle, which would have been horse-drawn had they possessed a horse, was packed so high with kit, that it looked as though at any minute the whole lot might fall to the ground. This fearful-looking load, it seemed, was to be pushed and pulled by a party of guards detailed for the purpose. We could understand the guards being in a hurry to get us outside, because the organisation of the whole outfit into some semblance of an ordered unit, must have taken at least an hour and a half. Finally, we were all ready to go and on the word of command from the German Major who was in charge of our cavalcade, we moved off slowly down the road.

The people with the horseless cart led the way, followed by a substantial body of Germans marching in a column, and then came the party of prisoners who were lined on each side of the road by a single column of guards. There were a further few files of *Luftwaffe* men behind us and bringing up the rear were all the small trucks with the kit and then the inevitable crowd of small children, who assembled as if by magic once the party got on the way. The morning was misty, which probably accounted for the extremely hasty departure. The general impression among the prisoners seemed to be that the American Armies were advancing towards Wetzlar from the direction of Frankfurt and if we had any luck at all, there was a good chance of our being caught up before the day was over.

Making a nice steady pace of about $2^1/_2$ miles an hour, we swung down the hill into Wetzlar. The whole population on Wetzlar seemed to have turned out to see us go by, some of them obviously under the impression that we were the American Army moving in. Heaven alone knows what some of these misguided people thought when the American troops actually did come along, for the effect, as in due course we were to learn, was very little short of devastating. Wetzlar had been very heavily and recently bombed and we proceeded with great difficulty over some of the roads, which were blocked by craters, and which were very muddy and slippery, even on those parts that were actually undamaged. We did not, at any rate, have to worry about being attacked by civilians as we had done so many times during that part of our 'tour' spent with Karl and Adolf.

We marched on and on. There was obviously a great desire by the Germans to place as big a distance as possible between themselves and the Dulag, and as long as everybody was fresh, they saw no purpose in stopping. It would have been about 6.30 a.m. when we left the camp and we must have walked for nearly three hours before we had our first break, which was a compulsory one, due to the presence of Allied aircraft overhead. During the break, the chief concern of a lot of the fellows was to make more adequate provision for the carrying of their Red Cross parcels. Some who had been members of the permanent staff at the camp, had managed to provide themselves with proper kitbags and they lost no time in ripping open their cardboard boxes and stowing the contents away. Others unloaded their blankets and stuffed the tins of food etc., in the ends in the approved way, but they were soon to find that this method had every possible disadvantage. I thought that I would leave my food where it was for the time being.

The raid over, we moved on once more. Apart from a brief halt to obtain water from a farm house, we made no further pause until around 12 noon, by which time we must have covered about 15 miles and we were all quite tired and extremely footsore. We dispersed into the woods and there was a brisk demand for can openers and penknives, or anything at all that would enable tins to be opened and inroads to be made into the stock of provisions. It all looked very nice, laid out in neat cardboard boxes. There were several tins of meat and other items such as biscuits, prunes, margarine, cigarettes etc. In fact, there was everything that was necessary to make up a tasty meal, if only we had possessed the necessary grounding in the form of either bread or potatoes. Whilst the biscuits served the purpose for the moment, it was obvious that if the march was going to be a long one, something would have to be done. Eating tins of salmon and such items entirely on their own was not only extremely wasteful, but quite likely to make the men feel ill, without really satisfying their hunger.

It was about this time that I first became friendly with Guy, who was a young fair-haired wireless operator. I did not learn his surname, but gathered that he had baled out on a raid on Köln a few weeks beforehand, and as far as he knew, he was the only member of his crew to survive. He did not appear to have any immediate friends in the party and as he and I seemed to get along, we soon started to spend most of our time together. I suggested to him (and to me it seemed a very obvious course of action, although Arthur had already declined the scheme) that we pool all our rations, with a view to making them go as far as possible. He agreed, of course, and it really was common sense, because the tins of meat or fish were better eaten as soon as it they were opened and there was easily enough in any of them to make a good meal for two people. We discussed the problem of carrying our goods and finally hit upon the notion of using an item of clothing to make a kitbag. I made a rapid change of the long-legged service issue pants, for the ones I had washed. Then tying up the legs of the former, I found that they made a practical kitbag, which could be carried like the traditional tramp's bundle on the end of a stick pushed over the shoulder

Everybody was trying to grapple with the same problem in his own way. The blanket idea was a dead loss from the start and obviously so, chiefly on account of the amount of space that was needed in order to get the things into the blanket in the prescribed fashion. (This actually was the only one by which they could be more or less relied upon not to fall out, as soon as the pack was slung over the shoulder.) It seemed that one could use the blanket to carry stuff in, or one could use it to keep warm at night, but only in the rarest circumstances was it likely to be of any practical use for both purposes. Some fellows still persisted, but I think that by the end of twenty-four hours at any rate, nearly everbody had to devise some separate means of carrying his goods and chattels.

Much to our relief, the interval for lunch was prolonged by at least an hour owing to the presence of a team of roving Thunderbolts, who kept coming down to have a suspicious little peep at our contingent, no doubt wondering whether we were all we seemed to be. We were ordered to retire into the deepest recesses of the woods, where the trees were so close together that the chances of stray machine-gun bullets penetrating were very remote. It all helped to give us the rest we needed and we were duly grateful to our friends up above!

At length, at about 2.30 p.m., a further count was taken by the guards, and we pushed on. We had begun by this time, to be acquainted with the two English-speaking guards who between them, issued all our orders. There was one whom we called Claude, who wore glasses, and who spoke in a very precise, though slightly broken English accent. We did not like him very much and we were to learn that he could be very bad-tempered. The other one we nicknamed Joe. His English was deep and somnolent, and completely lacking in intonation. It was he whom we had heard shouting up and down the passage at the time that we were getting ready to depart.

The afternoon was hot, and the pace got slower and slower. We crossed the main road from

Marburg to Giessen, along which we had recently bowled in such good style with Adolf and Karl in the open truck, and got into well wooded and rather more hilly country on the other side. The halts for a rest became more frequent, due, we suspected, to the fact that the Jerries in charge of the wagon that ought to have had a horse found it so difficult to get up even the smallest hill without falling well behind. Not only did we have to wait for them to catch up, but they also would be in such sore straits when eventually they breasted the rise, that the pause had to be extended to enable them to recover. Our guards, too, were quite good about arranging for us to have a drink of water at some of the many villages we passed through. The system in force seemed to be, that Joe would borrow the Major's bicycle and push on ahead. By the time the main force caught up again, several cottagers would be at their doors with pails of water ready for us to imbibe. Our chief difficulty for the moment was drinking vessels, but already some who had empty tins saved from lunch, were pressing them into service.

The most noticeable feature in all these villages was the extreme friendliness of the inhabitants, who could not move quickly enough to make sure that we had sufficient water. At one cottage a young girl threw out a handful of apples, which were readily grabbed by those who were nearest. When one of the Americans handed up a couple of packets of cigarettes, the lass disappeared and came back in a few moments with a whole basket full of the fruit, which she showered into our eager arms below. I managed to secure one of this second issue, and mighty good it tasted, too. There was the usual complement of white flags hanging from the windows. As in Wetzlar, I felt sure that before they had established our identity. Many of the villagers thought that the victorious Allied armies were marching in.

At last, tired and footsore, we stopped in the small town of Allendorf and were led into the school yard. It would have been about 5.30 p.m., and already it was beginning to grow chilly. We wondered if any arrangements were in force to enable us to get under cover. It came, therefore, as an agreeable surprise when we were ordered to file into the school room, which turned out to be a clean, reasonably warm apartment. It had obviously been used before for the same purpose, for two of the sides were lined with straw to a depth of about six feet. Being among the first in, I was lucky enough to secure a berth on the straw; I saved a place for Guy, and soon we were inspecting our stock of tinned goods to see what should be our choice for the evening meal.

Selecting a moment when there were no Germans in the room, Wing Commander Kelly, who was our senior officer, gave us a brief talk. He told us that we were marching too well, and if we wanted to slow this effort down, it was up to us to straggle as much as possible, and cause frequent halts to be made whilst those behind caught up. He also pointed out that our own common sense should dictate that our food would go further if parties of two or more arranged to share. He hoped that everyone would do this, as there was no means of telling how long we might be on the road. He doubted if even the Major knew where we were going to! The problem of bread was put to him, and he promised to see if anything could be done. Meanwhile, we were to go steady on the biscuits.

There was no light in the schoolroom, and we were warned that we ought to bed down by dusk. As we should probably be called before it was light, we should keep all our belongings handy, so as to avoid confusion when the time came to depart. It was then, that everyone who had not already done so, realised that his blanket, if it was doing duty as a haversack, was utterly useless as a means of keeping warm at night. Once unpacked (and the unpacking of it was most desperately easy), getting it packed securely again was next to impossible, for we were closeted in that little room like sardines in a tin.

CHAPTER THIRTEEN

Raising Our Hopes

By 8 p.m. we were all asleep, and compared with some of the nights spent in the train last week, we did not sleep so badly. However, there was many a loud grumble, when, about 1 a.m. the steady drone of Joe's voice could be heard repeating over and over again 'You must all get up – we are moving immediately.'

There were many who were inclined to say 'Oh, tickle him what's the big hurry?' and turn over and try to get to sleep again, but Joe was reinforced by Claude, and then by our own Wing Commander. Soon, the place was in a confused uproar in the darkness, there being no doubt that we had to go, and in some panic, too. Eventually, they got us out into the yard a count was made, and it was found that we were three short. Nobody seemed inclined to bother about it; I was destined to meet those adventurous three much later on, in Paris, and to learn exactly how they made good their escape.

We moved off, slowly – so very slowly that it was an effort, for those like myself who were not suffering from bad feet, to walk at such an unnatural speed. It was no faster than a funeral march, and as I feared, it deceived nobody, least of all Claude, who seemed to be the direct mouthpiece for the Major himself, the latter apparently speaking no English. An attempt was made to sort the party into two groups, those with foot trouble being allowed to proceed at their own pace, with a separate lot of guards. Wing Commander Kelly, who was among those who should have retired to the slow party, insisted that he would be alright, and that it was his intention to stay up in the lead, where he belonged.

We moved on but the pace of the fast party was no more rapid than it had been before, and in a few more minutes Claude had called a halt again, and proceeded to address us. It was obvious that he was wild with anger.

It is no use, the Major says that you must move more quickly. You, Wing Commander, I have asked you to go with those who are sick, and you have refused. But you must go faster – I myself will now go up in the front and you must all keep up with me – if you do not do so, it is sabotage, and you will all be dealt with as saboteurs. I do not say that if I were in your position I would not do the same, but it is sabotage, and we cannot allow it.

All this took time, of course, and our purpose, to some extent, was accomplished. However, there did not appear to be a great deal more we could do, and the pace took on a definite improvement. The number of genuine cases of bad feet, at this stage of the march, was no more than two or three. However, there was one poor red-headed fellow who definitely could not walk at all, and the last I saw of him he was sat on the Company's bicycle, being wheeled along by two of his comrades. I learnt afterwards that at the next village we came to he was left behind and taken into hospital. I hope it was true, for there were many more who dropped out later on, and whose fate I never did learn. To the crafty, labour-saving mind of the Germans, a quick bullet and no questions asked was always a likely way out of any difficulties such as these.

We made our first stop for water as soon as it was daylight, but we only had a short break, and were soon on the move again. It was difficult to determine the route we followed, for we invariably kept to very minor roads, and seemed to wind about all over the place, nevertheless making good a very rough track in a general north-easterly direction. Eventually, we were led into a spacious farmyard, where we settled down for our first meal of the day.

It was by no means too warm yet, for it would have been no later than 8 a.m. I made myself as comfortable as possible with Guy on a small heap of straw, with our backs to the door of a barn, and with a tin-opener borrowed from one of the guards, we opened a can of salmon for our breakfast. Some of the men had started the practice, soon to become insidious, of bartering cigarettes for bread from the guards. That morning, however, a small extra supply was obtained from the farmer, and an official issue of one thick slice per prisoner was made. There was no doubt about it, the American Red Cross food was extremely good. With a main dish of salmon, it was possible to follow up, as we did that morning, with prunes, and a little cheese, as well as bread and margarine. We felt that we had had a really good meal. Every parcel contained a tin of coffee and a large tin of powdered milk. With cooking facilities furnished by the farmer's wife, it was possible for a couple of our boys, who had acted as cooks back at the Dulag, to present a brew of coffee in the way that we liked it, far removed from the horrible black ersatz stuff that the Germans drank. The system too, had the advantage, that it took these willing lads an awful long time to brew coffee for eighty of us. We were therefore assured of a decent extension to our rest period!

And what had happened to the other four boys making up our original party of five? Well, Jack had become very friendly with an Australian Flight Lieutenant called Jarman, of whom we were to see a good deal more later on; Arthur seemed to be knocking around with Jack Evans, now the happy possessor of a stout pair of boots, and no longer troubled by his feet; and Diffy, his wounds now much better, was friendly with a small group of American officers. There were many others, too, among the crowd, with whom I speedily developed acquaintances. When marching, at any rate, it often became the case of passing the time of day and getting to know a bit about the fellow who happened to be next to me in the ranks.

The stay at the farm lasted about two hours. We found time to wash in the horse trough, and one fellow more proud of his appearance than the rest, was even seen to shave. Guy and I had the idea of cramming the whole of our kit into an old wicker basket that had we found lying around the yard, and then carrying the basket between us on a short length of wood garnered from the fuel pile. It seemed a good idea in theory, but in practice we found it far too heavy and unwieldy. We therefore abandoned the contraption before we had gone a hundred yards along the road. Another scheme three fellows seemed to be using successfully was to carry three lots of kit on a stout bamboo pole slung over the shoulders of two of them, thus giving one man a complete rest every third shift. They were not alone in devising weird and wonderful ideas for lessening the burden of kit carrying; there were hardly any two men shouldering their load in the same fashion – we must have looked a very odd crowd as we plodded along!

We were on our way again – the day passed very much in the manner of the previous one, with the inevitable two or three occasions when it was necessary to dive for the ditch to avoid the attentions of our comrades of the air, usually in Thunderbolts or Lightnings. Rumours were constantly being passed around that somewhere at the end of all this walking – it might be after 10, 20, or even 50 miles, nobody really knew – there would be a train that would whisk us speedily away to our destination. We original five smiled to ourselves at this talk, for we alone had up-to-date experience of the present state of the German railways. We knew that the train, even if it ever did materialise, might take us somewhere, but it certainly would not be speedily, and it was questionable whether it would even be to where we were supposed to be going! Our numbers, too, were steadily declining. In addition to the red-headed man, two others, one of them Wing Commander Kelly, were said to have been left behind in hospital that morning, and there seemed to be a few more familiar faces that were missing from the throng. A count, after one of our halts around noon revealed the present muster as seventy-four, but as had been the case in the early morning, those in charge seemed little inclined to worry. We suspected that a tally of the guards would show that there were no longer as many present as there had been when we started, but that was no business of ours.

It was nearly 2 p.m., and there was little sign of any pause for refreshment that day. Then, Joe in his sleepy monotone announced, 'We will march four more kilometres, and then we will eat and stop for the night'. This seemed far too good to be true, and the best pace so far was set by those in front, for the call of hunger was getting urgent. We must have walked nearer seven kilometres, for we kept up a cracking pace for over an hour, before we crossed the Frankfurt–Kassel *Autobahn*, and pulled up in the town of Nieder Gemünden. Once more, the Thunderbolts were busy overhead, and there was a long delay spent under what cover we could get, before our shelter for the night, another schoolroom, was located.

Bread, so necessary to make a decent meal out of our supplies of tinned goods, was now beginning to change hands for as many as twenty cigarettes for half a loaf, but there was little to be had even at that price. Those of us who were unlucky in the market, had to 'borrow' a slice from somebody more fortunate who might be willing to incur the risk of a very likely bad debt. Nevertheless, we knew we were very lucky to have the Red Cross parcels, and there was very little tendency to grumble. As in the morning, volunteers supplied tins of milk and coffee, and a good hot drink was prepared.

This schoolroom had deep recess windows, and perhaps mindful of the three who had escaped this morning, Claude announced that the first man to enter a window recess would be shot without question! There was no straw, but some of us who got there early enough were lucky in being able to find an extra blanket among a pile of old clothing, which looked as though it had been used for a dramatic performance at a recent date. Guy, who seemed remarkably good at rooting things out, organised for our use a bowl, a cup and a large soup ladle, which he broke in half saying that the handle could be used as a margarine spreader, and the bottom portion as an emergency drinking vessel. By arrangement, he took the bowl and I had the cup, which I carried down my battledress blouse, and served for me to drink out of for many a day afterwards. Somebody produced a couple of tubes of ointment for tired feet, and altogether the whole party settled down as cheerfully as possible to make the best of the conditions.

At 5 p.m. Joe entered, and with his characteristic 'Heil Hitler' gesture announced: 'You must go to bed now – at midnight we will move on.'

'Gets earlier every night,' I remarked caustically to Guy, 'Come on, let's get bedded down.'

We made ourselves as comfortable as possible underneath a table, and were soon asleep. We were woken after just three hours (for it was no later than 8 p.m. and barely dark) by Joe once more: 'You must all get up at once – we are marching immediately.' I wish it were possible to describe the exact sound of that fellow's voice – it just had to be heard to be believed. Every time he spoke it made one want to laugh, no matter how bad the news. Just a flat monotone was all he used, with no attempt at an accent on any word, however badly the English sense needed it.

So started what was to prove the most uncomfortable night we passed during the whole time we were over there – speaking, of course, for those of our original party. I have no doubt that many of the others who had been POWs a long time could tell many a grim tale. We seemed to be more or less going around in circles, for there were several long stretches of road, when from the position of the moon it was apparent that we were proceeding north-east and south in turn. There was a time when we must have walked for nearly two hours down a narrow valley, and the whole of the time we could hear shellfire so close on our right-hand side, that we estimated that the shells must be almost passing over our heads.

It was obvious from the excitement and chattering among the guards, that the war was getting too close for their liking. A powerful rumour spread among us that when we reached the main road, which was supposed to run along the end of the valley, we should find Americans already in possession, and our retreat cut off. It certainly needed some such inspiration to keep us going, for we were all getting to a state of great weariness. Odd disappearances were getting more rife – the horseless cart of kit seemed to have gone, and with it any number of guards. We seemed to be down to a mere handful, mostly old men, who probably thought that their best end was to get taken prisoner – and as quickly as possible. Claude, also, was no longer present, and the full brunt of the interpretation of the Major's wishes had fallen on Joe. Of our ranks, the number was down to a bare sixty-five, making a loss of seventeen since we started. What happened to most of them I just do not know, although if they had avoided getting shot, there is little doubt that sooner or later they would have made their way back to their own lines.

To add to the excitement were the additional rumours that the guards wanted to leave us all to our own devices and make good their escape, or alternatively that they wanted us all shot out of hand. This was a suggestion that the Major was reported to have refused point blank to countenance. It was all very mystifying and disturbing. We all wondered what the end of that road would bring, and whether the hour of our deliverance was at hand. But it was as yet only the small hours of Thursday morning, and this part of the story does not end until late on Friday afternoon … .

CHAPTER FOURTEEN

Free at Last!

The end of that valley brought us along to a bleak main road, along which we saw trundling in an easterly direction a solitary tank. For a moment it raised our hopes to the Heavens, only to sling them down again to rock bottom, as we realised that it was a Jerry. We flopped wearily on to the grass at the side of the road. It was about 2 a.m. and apart from the break of about four hours in the last schoolroom, we had been on the tramp for over a day. We could hardly remember when we had last eaten. We were done, and the reaction after having our hopes dashed was just sufficient to put us in the mood for mutiny.

It wasn't true, of course; we were nothing like at the end of our resources yet, and in a few minutes we were being forced to march on and taking it as calmly as we could in the circumstances. We fought our way slowly up a long gradual incline – every step was an effort, not only because of the pain in our tired feet, but also because of the difficulty of maintaining a straight course when one's every inclination was to close one's eyes and go to sleep. It seems a rather impossible, but a fairly credible tale was put out to account for the disappearance of one young lad, a paratroop hero from the ill-fated Arnhem expedition. Apparently, he had dropped off to sleep whilst on the march, had fallen in his tracks, and nobody had taken the trouble to pick him up.

Still we went on. We paused for occasional rests by the side of the road, but the night was cold. A great many of the men agreed with me that the effort of getting started again when cold and stiff after a halt of ten minutes, was far more trouble than the amount of rest to be obtained was worth. I think what kept me going was the pleasure of being able to take frequent nibbles at a slab of the very excellent chocolate included in the Red Cross parcel. I had quite a good supply, because being a non-smoker, I had traded some of my cigarettes for additional chocolate. I remember rationing myself to a bite from the bar every kilometre (nearly all the roads were plentifully supplied with 'kilometrestones'). This not only kept me supplied with energy, but also gave me something to anticipate, as we trudged along for kilometre after kilometre with no sign of a long rest being ordered. As for my feet, they were sore, but by no means as bad as most. My secret was plenty of soap well rubbed into the soles, and two pairs of socks worn at the same time, which was possible in my case, as my shoes were a little on the large size. I had real sympathy for the poor fellows who complained that the shoes issued to them in the Dulag were too small, because nothing more detrimental to comfort on a long march could be imagined.

Dawn was just breaking ahead on our right when at last we drew over on to the same *Autobahn* that we had crossed the night before at Nieder Gemünden. After walking along the magnificent highway for a couple of miles, we were taken to a kind of roadside canteen run by the German Red Cross. There were some who were too tired even to eat, and they just flopped on the floor with every appearance of being fast asleep as soon as their bodies touched the boards. Joe, meanwhile, was busy in the kitchen. To give him his due, he did all that was possible for us. 'You will get hot coffee,' came his dirge-like tones. Then, 'You will get hot soup – you will rest here two hours.'

'They could do with making it two weeks,' I muttered to Guy, sitting at a table beside me. 'What are we going to have for breakfast?'

We made that meal a good one, for the way these chaps wanted to force us along there was no telling when we might stop again. The fact that we had it all the wrong way round, with a meat course first, followed by coffee, and soup last, was not of the smallest consequence. As soon as we had finished, we settled ourselves with our heads on the table to try and secure a little sleep. It was only a bare forty winks, because the soup and coffee had taken some time to prepare, and Joe had us up and outside again well within the two hours he had allotted. The rumour was rife again that there would soon be a train. This time there seemed some foundation for it, because we had noticed two railways running into the fairly large town of Alsfeld, which was over on our left, and we had even spotted the smoke from a distant engine. What this party lacked was somebody like Adolf to make persistent enquiries as to the location and condition of the *bahnhofs*, and the possibility of transport!

Any real hopes we might have entertained were soon dashed, when we resumed our march and found that Alsfeld and the *Autobahn* were slipping away to our left, and we were off once more down the quietest of country lanes. Joe assured us that we would march 'only three more kilometres' and then we would find shelter. But we knew his kilometres of old, and were not at all surprised to find that it was 10 a.m., and the sun was riding high, before we at last pulled up in the village of Udenhausen, where provision was being made for us to rest in a barn at the side of the road.

'You will get more straw,' said Joe, bustling about as usual, trying to make sure that everybody was comfortable. Sure enough, somebody was detailed to go up into the loft and heave down great armfuls of extra straw to those waiting below. It was not a very big barn, and there was an abominable draught coming through various chinks in the door and walls, but in due course everybody had found a comfortable berth and was fast asleep. Fatigue such as we knew, could have but scant regard for such minor inconveniences as draughts and the cold stone floor.

It was probably due to these factors, and also because the sun shining through the cracks made the inside of the barn very light, that nobody seemed much inclined to sleep after about 2 p.m. By this time, most people had drifted outside, where it was considerably warmer than it had been indoors. The trade in bread for cigarettes was brisker than ever, as more and more of the guards realised our position, and I suppose, quite naturally, decided that they might as well make what they could out of it. Our Commanding Officer was now the other Wing Commander (Whose name I never knew). As the American Major was among those who had fallen by the wayside in the night, it appeared that Diffy was second in command, and presumably liable to be called upon to take over at any moment.

The Wing Commander addressed us on two points:

In the first place, I would advise everybody who can possibly keep going at all, to stay with the main body. Once you fall out, it's just a toss-up what they will do to you. You may get slung into some deep dungeon, and even if we do get overtaken, it may be weeks before anyone is able to find you. Secondly, we must make an effort to 'peg' the price of bread; if we don't these Jerries are going to force it up and up as our need grows, and in a very little while none of us will have either bread or cigarettes. Some of you are giving as many as forty cigarettes for a loaf of bread, and I tell you that it is far too many, and that twenty is plenty.

The first part of his advice was good, and I had no quarrel with it. The second part to me, provided a very interesting little study in economics. It is all very well to try and introduce a price control, but when there is no ready means of enforcing it, and the only law in operation is that of necessity, or supply and demand, it is hard to see how it can be expected to work. I, along with several others, did not smoke, and we (Guy and I) probably had anything up to a couple of hundred cigarettes apiece (the people at Dulag had been very generous just before we left). The only value those cigarettes had to us was what they would buy in terms of goods that we could use, which at the moment took the form of bread.

Had bread been plentiful, it would have been alright, and the Germans could have been offered five cigarettes, which was about the intrinsic value of a loaf, and if he refused, told to keep it; but bread was scarce, and the guards were cunning enough to hawk their odd bits around until they found the highest bidder. Was it any wonder that if a man with no bread had plenty of (to him) useless cigarettes, he was going to offer them pretty freely to the first Jerry he found with bread for disposal? To my mind, the Wing Commander went the wrong way about solving this problem. What should have been done was for the available cigarettes to have been pooled, and used to buy the bread on offer at a fair price, then an issue made to each man on a ration basis. As it was, we had the highly unsportsmanlike, and un-British, sight of many men being entirely without bread whilst others, more fortunate, had a plentiful supply, which they had picked up at varying prices.

At 3 p.m. we moved on. However, a count at this time numbered fifty-nine men – twenty-three had gone missing in just over two days. It was impossible to say exactly what were the losses among the guards, but at a very round estimate I should think that we started with well over 200, and that now there could not be more than about thirty at the most – such was discipline in the *Luftwaffe!* All the panic seemed to have gone out of the expedition and we sensed that if there had been any danger the night before, of being overrun by the advancing armies, it was considered, by now, to have passed. Joe announced, 'You will march only five kilometres, and then you will stop and have a complete night's rest'. So little faith had we in the amiable Joe's promises that there was a burst of derisive laughter at this remark. Nevertheless, we completed an uneventful 3 miles. Then, after hanging around in the village of Grebenau for an hour or so, we were taken, at 5 p.m., into another barn.

It was a slightly bigger barn, and boasted a small electric light, which to our surprise worked. Joe was as indefatigable as ever with his offers of 'more straw', and the promise of coffee now and soup in the morning. As had been the case at Undenhausen, we had strict orders that there was to be no smoking in the barn, but he need not have worried too much about that order being disobeyed. With the price of bread as it was, nobody felt he had any right to waste a cigarette by merely smoking it!

Guy and I found a billet underneath a plough, which offered us rather more room than most, because the various odd bits of the plough sticking out made it impossible for anybody else to get very near! It was whilst resting thus, that I made acquaintance with the brother of a very old friend of mine, whom I had met in the RAF, on the very first day I joined. It made it seem a very small world, meeting this fellow right out there in the wilds of the Third Reich. It was only the accident of his overhearing a chance remark to Guy about a training camp that we had both been at, that caused us to get into conversation.

Needless to say, we had a good deal to talk about, especially when I learnt that his fiancée lived in my own home town, and that they were hoping to get married as soon as we got clear of this country.

Sleep came better that night, and it really was a surprise to find, on waking, that it was daylight outside. Moreover, unlike the experience in the two schoolrooms, there was no immediate signs of our guards wanting to hurry us on. We had a leisurely breakfast, washed down by our own excellent brew of coffee. Then Joe made his first speech of the day: 'We are staying here until 2 p.m.' he said, to our intense stupefaction. 'At 11 a.m. you will get soup.'

'And you can walk round the yard for exercise,' added one wag.

'The war must be over,' said another, more optimistic than most.

'The point probably is,' I said to Guy, 'that the ruddy guards are a jolly sight more tired than we are, and the old Major knows, that the way he is going on he'll have no guards left at all in a couple of days. They're all old men and thoroughly fed up.'

Anyway, we were all very glad of the extra rest, for now that our bodies had stiffened up, it was astonishing how tired we really felt. Guy's feet, too, were giving him a lot of trouble, and although I recommended trying an extra pair of socks, he said that his boots were not big enough to allow it. We fell to taking stock of our remaining food, and decided that with great care we should have enough to make ample meals for another four days. It seemed a reasonable provision at the time, and one at any rate that did not warrant any stringent rationing. However, reading since, of bodies of prisoners who were marched around Germany for six or more weeks, I have often wondered what would have happened if things had not turned out as they did. We exchanged sixty cigarettes for a box of prunes surplus to one man's requirements. Immediately afterwards, we were offered another one by a man who had lost his false teeth and couldn't eat them. After a consultation, we suggested forty cigarettes only, as the market had slumped, and with many a loud grumble he handed them over! It struck me at the time as being awfully mean, but the laws of supply and demand in a world that knows only barter, are inexorable. Where this poor chap made his mistake was in offering a box of prunes to men that had just bought one. He should have looked around to try to find somebody whose need for prunes was greater than ours!

After we had finished stocktaking, I went outside to try and secure a wash. Eventually finding my way into a stable where there was a tap, I enjoyed pleasant ablutions while also enjoying the nice friendly aroma of horse. I even managed to borrow kit from a guard, and indulged in my fourth shave in fifteen days. I was surprised that I could muster sufficient spirits to chuckle at the thought of all the shaves that I had 'done' the RAF out of since I left my base a fortnight yesterday morning! It was about 10.30 a.m., and I was back in the barn instructing Guy where he could get a wash, when Joe came in and told us that there had been a charge in the plans. 'You must all get packed up at once,' he said. 'You will get your soup at 11 a.m., but we are marching again at a quarter to twelve, and you must all be ready to go.'

'The war's on again,' I remarked. 'Never mind, as long as they keep pushing us along, it's a fair indication that they're afraid of something.' We set about the task of getting our belongings together.

We had seen them making the soup out of potatoes and peas, and we were eagerly looking forward to the dish, which had just been placed outside the barn in a huge vessel that looked like a dustbin, when Joe dropped his second bombshell that morning. 'You must all get outside at once, we are marching immediately.'

'Not before we've had our soup!' was everybody's immediate reaction. But those fellows, once they got a bee in their bonnet, stood no nonsense. Two-thirds of the soup must have been left, only those, and Guy and I were among them, who were in an early part of the queue being lucky enough to get any. In most cases it had to be eaten, as expeditiously as possible, marching along the road.

It was an eventless march. The total distance according to Joe was 'only 15 kilometres', Soon after we started it commenced to rain for the first time since Monday, and only for the second time since we had been in Germany. It rained very hard, and we were all soon very wet. I remember hoping dismally that it would stop raining before we stopped marching, as otherwise I had visions of spending an even more uncomfortable night than the many we had passed already.

The countryside, looking fresh and green in its first moist covering, was more picturesque than any we had encountered since the early days with Karl and Adolf. I wondered if we were getting back into something like the same district, although, like everybody else, I had very little idea where we were. We made two stops only for water, the second of these at Niederjossa, by which time the rain had mercifully ceased, and the sun was doing its best to shine. I had been walking with Guy all day, and we sat down on a pile of logs, taking our last drink of water together – for I never saw him again. All subsequent enquiry as to what happened to him in the eventful hours that followed proved fruitless. I have made attempts to trace him since I returned to this country, but only knowing his Christian name, and not even being able to remember his unit, I have had no success. He just disappeared into the blue and whether he managed to outlive that memorable Good Friday, and return to tell his own tale, I shall never know.

We had five more kilometres to travel from that last stop at Niederjossa, and we were all, once more, beginning to feel uncommonly weary. The road here was marked off by a stone every 100 metres, which meant ten to the kilometre. Nearly everyone was reduced to counting and anticipating the stones as they came up, in an effort to occupy their minds. My chocolate supply was becoming reduced and my self-imposed rationing had stiffened up to a bite every kilometre and a half! Even the sight of a small Piper Cub 'spotter' plane hovering around over the low hills on our left, failed to arouse the excitement that it would have done, had we realised what its purpose was.

We derived some faint amusement at the sight of the Wehrmacht advancing to do battle, moving in the opposite direction to us. The contingent consisted of a motor car towing about ten men and their equipment on bicycles, a spectacle no doubt calculated to put the fear of God into the hearts of any enemy troops that might be encountered. Poor misguided German soldiers – I suppose many would never know what it was that they had been sent out to fight. I'm quite sure that I never realised the colossal might of the Allied armed forces until I saw a little bit of it in action for myself.

Even when the same cavalcade passed us again, now going the same way as we were, we were too absorbed with our 'kilometre stones' to take a great deal of notice, or to attach much importance to the event. The stones told us that we had but a bare kilometre to cover, and that, to us, was all that mattered. We were just coming up to the first houses of what looked like a reasonable sized town, and we could see the *bahnhof* over on our right and just pick out the name Niederaula. The air was very still, and I can clearly recall my last reflection as a POW. I didn't much fancy this time of the day, with the sun shining, to be coming into a town with a railway station. I had seen too much of what could happen to such places in a very short time, and the absence of aircraft in the sky had gone on so long that it must surely be due to be broken at any minute!

Then the miracle happened! An excited chatter broke out among the guards. There was a sudden sharp rat-a-tat-tat behind us, which could only be caused by machine-gun fire. We heard a loud insistent clatter from the rear, and we did not have to look to learn that it was caused by the approach of a tank. We looked wonderingly at our guards. It couldn't be – it wasn't possible – but they were all smiles. With shouts of 'Comrades', they were already throwing their arms on the ground or handing them over to anybody who would take them.

'Take cover' the sharp voice of our CO was getting control over the situation. 'The first tanks may be Jerries – they may be our boys, but they may shoot first, and ask questions afterwards!'

We dodged into a little pathway separating a house from its garden. There were two whole linefuls of clean white linen hanging out to dry. We grabbed the lot (I don't know what the poor housewife thought, she certainly never showed up to object). We stood in little groups waiting and wondering, and holding our tokens of surrender above our heads. The first tank was less than quarter of a mile away, and the machine-gun fire was getting more insistent.

'One man into the roadway, only' ordered the CO. I don't know who did the job, but he was presumably a brave man, although we learnt in a few minutes that we need not have worried. They knew we were there because unknown to us up at the front, our party had straggled out, and those behind had already established contact. They were our boys alright, bright-faced, fit, happy and smiling Americans, and never did Americans look so good!

The first few tanks and jeeps did not stop, their occupants being content to smile and wave to us. In about a minute, a jeep pulled in, and a jolly laughing captain got out. Although it took us a while to fully realise the fact, we were free men. Free! Free!

CHAPTER FIFTEEN

The Journey Back

We were in a spearhead. The Fourth Armored Division of General Patton's Third Army, had advanced that day only along that road. We were in the right spot at the right time. It was almost as though from the start of their tremendous sweep they had set out to catch up with us. They had commenced the drive on 15 March, the very day on which my crew baled out. In fifteen days they had pressed forward from the area north of the Moselle river on the west side of the Rhine, over the Moselle, then round and over the Rhine south of Koblenz. They had then rolled on across the German plain, taking in Frankfurt in a mighty encircling movement from the south (only some twenty-four hours after we had left Oberursel). Finally, they had swung round north again and were now in a headlong dash, with Berlin as their avowed first stop. It was Good Friday and it was a miracle, and nobody, not even those who would normally scoff at such an idea, was disposed to dispute it.

For the three hours that elapsed between our liberation and dusk, the mighty armoured column swept on. For an hour or two, we did little but stand by the roadside and admire it. How the Germans with their puny little units trundling along on bicycles or pushing their gear in perambulators, ever had the audacity to try to oppose such a force was beyond our comprehension. There seemed to be no end to it – tanks, jeeps and armoured vehicles of all descriptions were interspersed with supply trucks. The stream pressed on, bonnet to tail, at a speed that left us praising the skill of the drivers. It appeared as though the entire American Army must have turned out for our benefit that afternoon – and we were only in a spearhead!

The actual fighting in that little town of Niederaula was soon over. There was a short sharp battle, when half a dozen tanks sheared off the roadway and trundled over a ploughed field to attack a beautifully camouflaged electric train that was creeping stealthily down from the valley on our left. It was all over very quickly, however, and some of the more adventurous spirits among the ex-prisoners (how quickly we came to object to being described as 'prisoners') went with the American soldiers to help take over the train. They soon returned with a case of wine, which was quickly opened to provide a fitting toast.

After that, it was a case of how soon can you get us home. No praise that I can offer can be too high for the manner in which those American lads made us feel welcome, and the way in which they organised our return under incredibly difficult conditions. Their trouble was that for the moment the traffic was going in the opposite direction. Also, at that time, though it must have become commonplace in the weeks that followed, handling liberated POWs was entirely new to them. There was no procedure laid down, but they knew that all we wanted was to get back home. Somehow or other, they meant to get us there, even if they had to stop the war to do it!

The journey back took a clear seven days, from the time we were liberated until we landed at Croydon on the following Friday afternoon. To attempt to describe our adventures in the same amount of detail as has been given up to now, would I fear, be an anti-climax. Nevertheless, we did have our full share of the fun, before we had the thrill of seeing our native land again.

That night, the Americans did not know quite what to do with us. Rather than leave us behind, they took us with them for about 15 miles to the point that had already been decided upon as their objective for the day. We passed the night in the best manner possible (I enjoyed the luxury of a berth in the front cab of a wagon) amid the roar and racket of the heavy gunfire. It kept us all awake most of the time, but we were far too happy to object to it. We did hope, though, that a stray shell from the other side would not fall on our encampment!

In the morning, the Americans surpassed themselves, laying on hot pancakes, syrup and a fresh orange for breakfast. As early as 8 a.m., three trucks had been organised to take our party out of the forward area, to a spot that would be rather more safe from the enemy. With a long break in the middle of the day, those trucks took us to a temporary German POW cage just outside Hanau. During the whole of that journey, our drivers had almost to fight their way through the still endless stream of American armed might that was pushing on behind the spearhead to consolidate the positions already taken. We were fed on American field rations that day, but a cooked supper was ready for us at night and we felt that life was good.

Hanau, like its sister town Giessen, was another place that had had a terrific pounding from the Allied bombers. Although we drove right through the middle of the place twice on our way to the POW cage (owing to the driver losing his way) and once on our way out, I did not observe a single building that could be considered fit to live in.

At Hanau (or rather the American camp just outside the town), we had a long hold-up, which tested the patience of many of the fellows. The delay was due to the transport difficulty, and whilst we were sure that the CO was doing all he could for us, we felt that he was handicapped because he did not know where to send us next.

There didn't seem to be anyone whom he could ask who would be likely to supply the answer. Rumour was divided between the speculation that we should proceed in trucks to Trier on the Luxembourg border and thence by aircraft to London, or that we should have to be sent first to some place that was vaguely described as 'down the road', where we have to be properly interrogated before we could be allowed to leave the continent.

During our stay at this place, which we reached on the Saturday evening and left about the same time on the Easter Monday, we were billeted in three or four private houses. It was expecting a lot to assume that we should all get beds, but I was lucky enough to share a single one with my old friend Harry, my fellow navigator, whilst two others slept on the floor in the same room. For all its shortcomings, we were unanimously agreed that this apartment was a big improvement on schools, barns or even the cabs of army trucks! The Americans did everything they could for our comfort in the way of food, chocoloate and cigarettes. It is recorded that one poor soldier of the British Army, who had joined our party from another source, and who had been a prisoner since Dunkirk, actually thought that the first slice of white bread given to him was cake!

The women occupants of our houses were very civil and made us as much at home as they could in the circumstances. They were all at their windows waving us farewell, when at last our contingent pulled out on our way again in the gathering dusk of Monday evening. There was a long hold-up waiting for a convoy to get clear of the pontoon bridge before we could cross the River Main, but once on our way, we made good speed. In less than an hour, we were driving through the ruins and desolation of the fine German city that had once been Frankfurt am Main. What a sin and shame that any so-called civilised nation should allow its cities and people to be so degraded. On a much larger scale, it was Giessen and Hanau over again, although one could spot an occasional building that had enough of it left standing to make it at least partly habitable. The extent of the damage, once again, would have to be seen to be believed but to give some idea, I would say that if one were to take a pocket handkerchief, and black out (say) a piece the size of a penny in the middle, that might represent the bomb damage to a city of comparable size in England (take Sheffield as a fair example); in Frankfurt, the piece the size of a penny could stand for the *undamaged* portion, and there you have the difference. It is no disparagement to the suffering that was Sheffield's, but a compliment to the might of Allied bombers. How the Frankfurters stuck it is beyond comprehension – to me it was wicked and sinful. I got tired of looking at it as we drove through the streets, but it was war.

There was a strong impression as we left the city that our destination was to be Oberursel, that pleasant little spot on the side of the hill that had some memories for we original five, and a great many more for those among the party who had been detained there at the time that the place functioned as Dulag Luft. Our five, incidentally, were now four, as Diffy had at last fallen victim to one of his head wounds, which had been slower than the rest in healing. The wound had finally, no doubt on account of the limitations of our diet and the lack of rest, festered and turned septic. He had retired into hospital at Hanau, along with our Wing Commander, who was reported to have influenza. We never saw either of them again. Our senior officer was now Jack's friend, Flight lieutenant Jarman. As the party was now really getting short of officers, it more or less fell to any of the few of us who remained to lend a hand where any organisation was required.

It was Oberursel alright, which was now, of course, in American hands. It was being used as a POW cage for the ever increasing inrush of German prisoners. We were subjected to a brief interrogation, and by and large, I doubt if they really wanted to see us. Whilst they offered us all they had during our stay of twenty-four hours, which included plenty of good food but no beds, I think they were quite glad to see us leave at about 8 p.m. the following evening. They had only been in the place themselves a couple of days, and badly wanted time to get organised without being bothered with such out-of-the-ordinary influxes as was represented by a party of some fifty-odd liberated POWs. Whilst we were here, Jarman got things cracking to the extent of drawing up a nominal roll of the party, an item which to my mind had been sadly lacking up to now (for with it I reckon I could have traced my friend Guy and perhaps been able to let his parents have a little information, if he was still listed as missing). Although the American Commander said that our next-of-kin would now be notified that we were safe, we thought it quite unlikely that any word would get through before we took it back ourselves.

The next stage of the journey was to be to a place called Stennay on the Meuse in France, which sounded an awful long way from the war and a whole lot nearer home. There were only two trucks to take fifty-eight of us, and we rode in the most fiendish discomfort for eighteen hours, with a halt for breakfast for a bare half hour in Trier. It wasn't really anybody's fault that for some reason or other Jack Evans got left behind at Oberursel, because a careful count when the trucks were loaded revealed the precise number that there should be. It was not until the following day that we found we had picked up another stray prisoner, who had been drafted on to our party at the last moment from an unknown source. What happened to Jack, is again unknown, and our little party of five was now down again to Jack Acheson, Arthur and myself, and we once more found ourselves drifting together.

Yes, it was a nightmare trip, but we were going home and that was all that mattered. Tired, stiff and weary, we climbed out of those wagons at yet another POW cage at Stennay. Once more, the people in charge were not expecting us, though they made every possible endeavour to secure our comfort during our brief stay there. For the first time since we joined forces with the Americans, the thirteen officers in the party found, thanks to the organisation of Flight Lieutenant Jarman, that we could enjoy the facilities of the Officers' Mess. The food that was served to us there was really tip-top. Throughout the whole of the journey back, I have nothing but the most unstinted praise to offer to the Americans and the manner in which they left no stone unturned to ensure that everything they had to offer (and it was not always very much) was ours for the time that we needed it.

We had our first night's sleep on a bed to ourselves that night. We awoke refreshed and eager to press on to dear old Blighty. An, extra truck was laid on, and we were told that the trip to Paris would be made under the auspices of their best and most experienced drivers, in a matter of six hours. As the distance was 200 miles, and it had taken us eighteen hours to travel 300 miles the night before, we were inclined to doubt this information. However, we had reckoned without the quality of the French roads, and the fact that traffic on them was practically non-existent. We tore along at breakneck speed, praying that we had not come through so much and covered all this distance only to finish up in a French ditch. But these drivers knew their job, and with a brief stay for lunch by the wayside, we finally drew into busy unbombed Paris at about 4 p.m., on a beautiful sunny afternoon, three weeks almost to the hour since we had left our aircraft, in such unceremonious fashion. It was, we reflected, a very easy matter to get into Germany, but getting out again had been the very devil of a job!

Paris was all bustle, and compared with the broken cities of the Reich, was full of gaeity and happiness, although we knew that beneath the surface there was a long tale of bitter suffering. Moreover, the people were by no means blessed, even now, when it came to the question of food. We had little time for all this, however, as our transport whisked us round to all the places that it seemed necessary for us to visit. A complete separation was made of Americans from British, and then of officers from other ranks. Thus we said goodbye to all our friends, Arthur included. There were now five of us, Jarman, Jack and myself, and Flying Officers Denis Wathieu, (a Belgian serving with the RAF) and Johnny Cranston, left to uphold the ranks of the British officers and return to England alone.

I had every reason to believe that we got there before anybody else – the first batch, almost, I should think of prisoners liberated by the advance of allied armies from the west (as distinct from the Russians from the east) to return to this country. There certainly could not have been many in front of us, at any rate. We were incredibly fortunate – we were billeted in a luxury hotel, the Bedford, had the supreme joy of a really hot bath, a most sumptuous repast (we learnt that the food came from America) and were able to anticipate the thrill of going to bed between sheets.

Meanwhile, we had the pleasure to meet a Major Parr whilst having our meal. He, learning that we had no money, very graciously stood us drinks all round. This gesture was very much appreciated, as was that of the English airman, who earlier in the afternoon had lent us the necessary ten francs to enable us to buy a cup of tea at a NAAFI canteen. We knew that we looked terribly scruffy, and that officers were not allowed in NAAFI canteens, but nobody dared to tell us so, and we needed that cup of tea awfully badly!

After our meal, our luck continued to hold. Quite by accident I got into conversation with a pilot of Transport Command, from whom I borrowed a pen to address a brief note to my wife (although I had every hope that I should reach home before the letter). He asked me who we were and what we were doing here. He enquired how we hoped to get back to England, and I said we had no idea yet. Then he announced that he was taking an empty Anson back tomorrow. It seemed too good to be true and we hardly dared hope, but this officer knew just the right people to sever any red tape that stood in the way. By 10 a.m. the next day everything was arranged for us to leave Le Bourget airport at 3 p.m., and there would even be transport to take us there.

All that I wanted now was a souvenir to take back home. The pilot of the Anson, obliging to the last, fixed up for me to exchange my 200 remaining cigarettes for a bottle of champagne at a little wine shop up a side street. I stowed this away among my kit, now no longer carried in the underpants, but in an old sack furnished by the obliging woman of the house in Hanau. Like the others, I could hardly wait for the afternoon – and dear old England.

The little Anson seemed like a toy after the mighty Lancaster, but we all got in quite comfortably, and were soon making good a steady two miles a minute into the wind and in a straight line for Dungeness. We crossed the coast dead on track, each one of us feeling his own particular thrill now that our big adventure was nearly over. Before 5 p.m., we had touched down on the grass runway at Croydon airport, where at last we were expected, and there was a rush of officials to meet us.

It took us another day to complete the formalities. Then it was a case, for me, at any rate, of saying goodbye to everybody then going as quickly as possible to base, and then home on leave to my folk, eagerly waiting and wondering!

Epilogue

There still remains to be told the sequel: the story that I was to hear a few hours after we landed at Croydon. We were taken from Croydon to London. I had little difficulty in securing permission to sleep elsewhere than in the quarters alloted, for I wished to visit my sister and allow her to be the first (after I had telephoned my wife) to hear the glad news. After she got over her shock (and the poor girl wept on my shoulder) she told me, to my intense surprise, what had hardly occurred to her that I did not know. The Skipper, Roy (the mid-upper) and Ray (the wireless operator) were all safe in England, and had not even baled out of the aircraft! From what I could gather, there had been some hitch due to Roy and Ray being off intercom after the order to 'Fix parachutes' and they had not heard the order to 'jump'. By the time they had got things sorted out between them, the danger from the fire appeared to have receded. The Skipper had then decided that a bit of distance towards safety could be made. Accompanied by another aircraft from the Squadron, he had eventually made a forced landing in Belgium, and with his depleted but safe crew, had returned to base two days later.

Jack's feelings when he heard this the next morning, were like mine, very mixed. However, the one thought that was uppermost in our minds was that poor old Ron was still missing, and unless and until he turned up, the story could have no happy ending. All that remains for me to add is that when I penned my earlier chapters there was no news at all of him. His poor wife, whom I knew quite well, was frantic with grief to think that everybody except the one who mattered so much to her had 'got away with it'. Fortunately, I do have a happy ending for this tale. While writing the manuscript for this book, the glad news came through that Ron was safe, well and back at home.

Appendix

I.S. 9.(W.E.A.)

WARNING AGAINST GIVING INFORMATION ABOUT YOUR ESCAPE OR HOW YOU EVADED CAPTURE

This applies to Members of all Services and continues even after discharge therefrom.

1. It is the **duty** of all persons to safeguard information which might, either directly or indirectly, be useful to the enemy.

2. The Defence Regulations make it an **offence**, punishable with imprisonment, to **publish** or to **communicate** to any unauthorised person any information or anything which purports to be information on any matter which would or might be directly or indirectly useful to the enemy.

3. This document is brought to your personal notice so that you may clearly understand information about your escape or how you evaded capture is information **which would be useful to the enemy**, and that therefore to communicate any information about your escape or how you evaded capture **is an offence under the Defence Regulations.**

4. You must not disclose the **names** of those who helped you, the **method or methods** by which you escaped, the **route** you followed or how you reached this country, nor must you even give information of such a general nature as the **names of the countries** through which you travelled. All such information may be of assistance to the enemy and a danger to your friends. <u>Be specially on your guard with persons who may be newspaper representatives.</u>

5. **Publishing or communicating** information includes :—

    (a) publication of accounts of your experiences in books, **newspapers** or periodicals (including Regimental Journals), **wireless** broadcasts or lectures :

and   (b) giving information to friends and acquaintances either male or female, in private letters, in casual conversations or discussions, even if these friends or acquaintances are in H.M.'s or Allied Forces and however " safe " you may consider them to be.

6. F.O. (557-44)
    A.C.I. (1896-43)   } prohibit lecturing by escapers or evaders to any unit without
    A.M.C.O. A89-44   prior permission of the Admiralty, War Office, Air Ministry.

TO BE COMPLETED IN THE PERSON'S OWN HANDWRITING.

    I have read this document and understand that if I disclose information about my escape, evasion of capture I am liable to disciplinary action.

Signed _Annett_   Date _5 - 12 - 45_

Full Name (Block letters) _SQUIRE SCOTT_

Rank and Number _P/O 1841324_

Unit _9 Squadron R.A.F. 5 Group_

Witnessed by _Stone Christopher_
Capt ac

WHAT YOU MAY SAY.

By signing the attached document you have undertaken to maintain a strict secrecy about your experiences. It is realised, however, that your family and friends are certain to ask you questions. *Below you will find suggestions for the best way of answering them :—*

ROYAL NAVY.

(In similar terms to those for Army and R.A.F., altered to suit particular circumstances.)

ARMY (Escapers).

I was captured by the Germans (Italians) and sent to a prison camp in **Germany (Italy)**. I managed to escape and get back to this country, but I cannot tell you how I did that without spoiling the chances of others who are trying to get away. *I am sure you will understand that I cannot tell you anything till after the war, and I have orders not to say more than I have already told you.*

or

ARMY (Evaders).

I managed to evade capture and get back to this country. As many others are trying to do the same, you will understand I cannot tell you anything till after the war. In any case, I have orders not to say more than I have already told you.

R.A.F. (Escapers).

I was shot down by flak during a bombing raid. I baled out, and was captured and sent to **Germany**. I managed to escape from a prison camp and get back to this country. As many others are trying to do the same, you will understand it is not possible for me to tell you anything till the war is over. In any case, I have orders not to say more than I have already told you.

or

R.A.F. (Evaders).

I was shot down by flak and baled out. I managed to evade capture and get back to this country. As many others are trying to do the same, you will understand it is not possible for me to tell you anything till after the war. In any case, I have orders not to say more than I have already told you.

Full Name (Block letters) SQUIRE SCOTT

Rank and Number P/O 184134   **Signed** Keith

Unit 9 Squadron R.A.F.   **Date** 5. 4. 45
5 GROUP

Witnessed by Ron Christopher
Capt AC

Squire 'Tim' Scotts 1944–5 Operations

OPERATIONS

1944

July	24	Donges (N)	5.30
	25	St Gd (D)	4.05
	26	Gwors (N)	8.55
	28	Stuttgart (N)	8.00
	29	Avkagne (D)	4.40
Aug	9	La Rochelle (D)	6.15
	10	Bordeaux (D)	{3.40 (N) 3.45
	11	Givors (N)	8.20
	12	Brest (D)	4.40
	18	La Pallice (D)	6.25
	24	Ijmuiden (D)	3.20
	27	Brest (D)	5.00
Sept	11	Archangel (N)	10.40
	15	Tirpitz (D)	7.15
	16	Return N	11.00
Oct	11	Flushing (D)	2.48
	15	Sorpe Dam (D)	5.32
	17	W. Kapelle (D)	2.40

1944
Oct 19   Nuremberg N 7.20
   29   Tirpitz   D {8.15
                         N {5.00

Nov 26   Munich   N 9.45
Dec 8   Urft Dam   D. 5.30
   11   Urft Dam   D   6.25
   17   Munich   N   9.35
   18   Gydnia   N   9.40
1945
Jan. 12   Bergen   D   7.10
Feb 3   Ijmuiden   D   2.50
    6   Altenbecken D   5.45
       7–4   Ems Canal   D   4.30
March 3   ✓   ✓   ·N   5.15
     13   Arnsberg   D   6.40
     14   ✓   D   6.22
     15   ✓   D   5.30